T0383182

ACHIEVING PATIENT
(aka Customer)
EXPERIENCE EXCELLENCE

Lessons From a Successful Cultural
Transformation in a Hospital

ACHIEVING PATIENT
(aka Customer)
EXPERIENCE EXCELLENCE

Lessons From a Successful Cultural
Transformation in a Hospital

Rhonda Dishongh • Qaalfa Dibeehi
Kalina Janevska • Gregory D. Erickson

CRC Press
Taylor & Francis Group
Boca Raton   London   New York

CRC Press is an imprint of the
Taylor & Francis Group, an **informa** business
A PRODUCTIVITY PRESS BOOK

MIX
Paper from
responsible sources
FSC® C014174

CRC Press
Taylor & Francis Group
6000 Broken Sound Parkway NW, Suite 300
Boca Raton, FL 33487-2742

Library of Congress Cataloging-in-Publication Data

Achieving patient (aka customer) experience excellence : lessons from a successful
    cultural transformation in a hospital / authors, Rhonda Dishongh ... [et al.].
        p. ; cm.
    Includes index.
    ISBN 978-1-4665-8308-5 (hardcover)
    I. Dishongh, Rhonda, 1968-
    [DNLM: 1. Patient Satisfaction--Personal Narratives. 2. Cultural
Competency--Personal Narratives. 3. Hospital-Patient Relations--Personal Narratives. 4.
Organizational Case Studies--Personal Narratives. W X 158.5]

    362.11068'5--dc23   2012050578

Visit the Taylor & Francis Web site at
http://www.taylorandfrancis.com

and the CRC Press Web site at
http://www.crcpress.com

Contents

Dedications and Acknowledgments

Rhonda Dishongh's Dedications

There are many people who have made me who I am and continue to shape me into a better me. I would like to thank my parents, Kenneth and Elaine Spann, who always gave me the courage to be different and to take chances. They have been proud of me and given me opportunities they did not have. My sister, her husband, and my beautiful niece and caring nephew—Laura, Gregg, Sarah, and Gregory, respectively—never have to say a word because just being there has spoken volumes. My brother, Kenneth Spann, makes me feel protected even to this day. Stephen Nunenmacher has shown me that doing what is right is always more important than self-gain. It has also been his incredible music and lyrics that have served as my muse during some late nights of writing. Julie Nunenmacher exudes grace and resilience in her very character and has taught me the importance of those characteristics; their baby, Jude, lights up my life.

I would like to thank my staff and peers, past and present, from whom I have learned everything I know. Karen Haney, George Gaston, and Keith Parrott gave me my first chance in Patient Experience; Louis G Smith, Jr., and Linda Stephens every day provided encouragement, guidance, and acceptance of my big, big, big ideas. Helen Powers told me I could do anything and insisted I believe it. Thanks to John Murray for always being a phone call or text away and Greg, Qaalfa, and Kalina for always putting up with the weird way I see the world.

Most of all, thank you to my husband and children, who have waited at dinner for me or let me work late into the night and early in the morning. Drew is a beautiful, passionate young man who has already made a big difference in our world at eighteen years of age. I cannot wait to see him leave his mark on the big world. Steven shows compassion and caring in all of his interactions, even on the football field. I respect his opinion, and I am so glad he is confident in sharing it. Rachel, who will always be my baby girl, makes my heart sing. She is so smart and accomplished and knows no fear. My husband, Malcolm, has been by my side and in my heart forever. We met as teenagers, and I do not know what I would do without him. These five people have been my constant support and have truly made this come true.

I would like to dedicate my portion of this book to my grandmother, Ruby Jean Dixon. Without her example of loving and taking care of the masses, I would not be who I am. I dedicate my career to making her proud every day.

Qaalfa Dibeehi's Dedications

I dedicate this book to those who helped me in my own transformation by motivating and engaging me, holding me accountable, and recognizing my talents: Mom, Dad, Rock Brailsford, Mrs. Thigpen, Lt. Col. Willie Bratcher, Prof. David Morse, Prof. Philip Ramsey, Dr. Cordia Beverley, and Yumiko Ogawa. Thanks to the institutions that have been important backdrops in my life: Memorial Hermann Hospital, Law Elementary School, Texas Children's Hospital, Johnston Jr. High, Lamar Sr. High School, Houston Community College, State University of New York–New Paltz, City University of New York, the City of New York, New York University, Metropolitan College, Beyond Philosophy, and the City of London. Thank you to my coauthors and friends: Rhonda, for being what Patient Experience is all about; Kalina, for the therapeutic camaraderie and feedback; and Greg, for being the best Patient Experience convert ever.

Kalina Janevska's Dedications

I dedicate this book to my parents, Vlado and Vesna Janevski, and sister, Dafina Janevska, for inspiring my life choices and showing me continuous care and nurturing.

Qaalfa Dibeehi has given me opportunities and pushed me to develop my talents so that the future Kalina can admire and be proud of the present Kalina he helped grow.

A sincere thank you to Rhonda and Greg for self-lessly sharing their story and making me part of it.

And finally, a thank you to the people in my life who have inspired and motivated me to give more and be more: my friends, my teachers, and my family.

Gregory Erickson's Dedications

There are many people who I would like to acknowledge who have helped me along the way. I start with my brother, John Christopher Erickson, who has been by my side through this entire journey called life. My best friend, who started as my brother in the Navy, Jim Brekhus always believed in me and showed me a good time. Thank you to my in-laws: Raymond, for stepping into the role my father had to leave too soon, and Nelda, for always making sure I justified my reasons.

My professional career was formed with the help of many individuals but none so much as Louis Smith and Heath Rushing, understanding leaders who held me as accountable as I held others. Jessica Wooten was my balance that made success easier. Derek Hebert and Stephanie Foster were my comrades at work on many occasions.

My wife of more than twenty years, but my purpose for twenty-four, Stephanie Erickson, gave me direction and strength. My son, Trenton, has shown me that he can do anything that he sets his mind to. My belief in him has given me the courage to believe in myself. Kadyn, my youngest son, has the energy and passion for life that I wish I had. If I am half the father to them that they are sons to me, it is an amazing feat.

I would like to dedicate my portion of this book to my father, John Erickson, who was taken away from this world when I was only sixteen. It was the circumstances of his death that gave me the direction I needed in life. It was the person that he was along with my mom, Nelda Joan Erickson, who has gone to be with my father, who gave me who I am and the power to be anything I want to be.

Preface

Patient Experience management has always been a part of healthcare work since interacting with patients has always underlined giving consideration and care to their experience to varying degrees. However, until now, Patient Experience has been left to what we can call an intuitive style of management. This means that the nature of the experience delivered has been heavily determined by a mix of circumstantial factors mainly related to the individuals behind the experience management's personal interpretations, the employees' moral compass, and current resource restrictions that affect ad hoc decisions. As a result, two basic problems arise:

- The Patient Experience effectively becomes a series of individual transactions even though the patient perceives the experience as a whole. The end result is that the patient is often confused, frustrated, and alienated by the inconsistent experience.
- Well-meaning healthcare professionals can all be fully intent on delivering the best possible Patient Experience, but they do not really appreciate how to calibrate the experience they deliver with that of others or even know what a great Patient Experience is beyond a good clinical outcome.

With the Hospital Consumer Assessment of Healthcare Providers and Systems (HCAHPS) firmly in place in the United States, efforts to manage the Patient Experience became mandatory and business justified. Reimbursement to hospitals is now partially dependent on how well patients feel they have been treated. Naturally, that puts Patient Experience management at or near the top of the priority list for hospitals.

In the United Kingdom and Europe, patient satisfaction has been a matter of attention since the 1990s, being widely accepted as an outcome measure in trials testing new drugs or interventions as well as a measure of quality of care.[*] In the United Kingdom, the National Health Service (NHS) 2010–2015 plan highlights

---

[*] Delnoij, Diana M., Measuring patient experiences in Europe: What can we learn from the experiences in the USA and England? *European Journal of Public Health*, Vol. 19, No. 4, 354–356, 2009. Published by Oxford University Press on behalf of the European Public Health Association.

the need to significantly expand the measurement of patient satisfaction and links significant portions of provider income to Patient Experience. This means, for the first time, connecting the level of patient satisfaction with hospital income. Over time, up to 10% of hospital income could be dependent on patient satisfaction.[*]

Unfortunately, this new high priority does not readily translate into guaranteed collaboration, understanding, or clarity of action for executives, managers, or other employees within hospitals. In fact, for many it became a difficult task of balancing lofty goals with budget, time, and resource capacity restraints. It would be no issue to achieve the highest marks if the organization could freely invest time and resources to focus on getting those goals achieved. However, reality requires a more skilled juggling effort among the clinical, business, and experience aspects of hospital work. Moreover, it requires a different kind of mindset, decision-making model, and overall approach to how employees behave within the organization. This different approach should naturally and intuitively lead to an optimum balance between patient satisfaction and business benefit when put into practice on a daily basis. In addition, this will allow, enhance even, the best clinical outcomes.

Putting both business and Patient Experience knowledge into action is the challenging part. Furthermore, that difficulty is compounded by the need to embed that culture across the organization such that it becomes "a way of being" rather than just another set of additional tasks to pile on the heap of existing programs and initiatives. Task orientation leading to ineffectual ongoing training, consultants, and projects that absorb money and effort is harmful, although it can appear to be forward moving simply because the language sounds good and the activity looks busy.

The original idea of this book was to help healthcare professionals understand the components required to build a customer-centric (i.e., patient-centric) culture and inspire action. It quickly became clear that the lessons that would make a patient-centric cultural transformation successful are similar to those that would make any customer-centric transformation successful.

In this book, we uncover how one such cultural transformation was successfully achieved in a hospital setting. As stated previously, the lessons learned can be applied anywhere (hospital, retail services, contact center, etc.) and in any industry (healthcare, telecommunications, financial services, etc.).

Rhonda and Qaalfa first worked together in 2005. Qaalfa was a consultant hired to help the hospital system improve its customer experience. That work was very successful. Since that time, Rhonda has applied the learning to a variety of hospitals within the system. Specifically, the system took over management of a community hospital (which we henceforth refer to as "Community General"), which had twenty years of inconsistent financial and patient satisfaction performance.

---

[*] The NHS 5 Year Plan. http://patientexperiencefeedback.com/measuring_patient_satisfaction/the_nhs_5_year_strategic_plan.html (accessed November 2012).

Rhonda was brought onboard at Community General to bring the magic that had helped improve other hospitals in the system.

This is the story of how Rhonda first and Greg as an ally worked with and led a team to create a culture in which things are not allowed to just happen but an experience is deliberately created. The story is told from the point of view of two people. However, the story was not created by those two alone. It took the efforts and knowledge of many leaders, support people, and frontline team members.

Rhonda Dishongh and Greg Erickson's story is a rich source of instructive lessons. Qaalfa and Kalina summarize the learning into several key points each healthcare manager should know and act on when creating a culture of service excellence.

For the remainder of the book, we use avatars to make it easy to identify whose point of view is being told:

Gregory Erickson

Kalina Janevska

Rhonda Dishongh

Qaalfa Dibeehi

In each chapter, we start with the story of what happened in the words of the Patient Experience practitioners, Rhonda and Greg, who lived it day in and day out. They uncover the situation as it unfolds, showing not only what they did but also why they did it and, importantly, what it felt like. Achieving a cultural transformation is hard work. It is not rocket science, but it is really easy to miss the key lessons because most people are so focused on the tactics to implement that they forget the intent of the tactics. Thus, Customer Experience experts Qaalfa and Kalina follow up each chapter's story with the key lessons.

We hope this book will help you start a change toward achieving Patient Experience excellence.

Let's begin … .

About the Authors

Rhonda Dishongh

While studying communication at Houston Baptist University, **Rhonda Dishongh** aspired to be a disk jockey for a heavy metal radio station. She began working as a registration representative in the emergency room of a hospital to earn extra money while in school. In those three years, she was bitten by the healthcare bug, forfeited the plan to be a disk jockey, and continued her career as a manager in the business office.

Interactions that occurred during her beloved grandmother's death inspired her to dedicate her career to designing desired experiences in healthcare. With twenty-five years of service at the various hospitals and system offices, Rhonda has been an instrumental part of the leadership team. Rhonda has contributed to teams' successful outcomes, receiving national recognition for performance in quality and customer experience. Rhonda continues to serve as the director of Customer Experience Design and Patient Business Services.

On a personal note, Rhonda has been married to her high school sweetheart for twenty years and spends her personal time documenting a pictorial history of her two sons and daughter.

Qaalfa Dibeehi

Qaalfa Dibeehi (pronounced "alfa dibay-i") is a recognized global expert in Customer Experience with more than twenty years of experience in the customer-related space with particular emphasis on the special problems and sensitivities of organizations that have a dual commercial and social/community responsibility.

He is the chief operating and consulting officer of Beyond Philosophy, the Customer Experience consultancy. He was previously a managing consultant with Round, the customer centricity consultancy. While there, he helped develop an assessment tool that eventually won a 2003 Customer Relationship Management (CRM) Innovation of the Year award. His experience also includes senior roles at Fulcrum Analytics, where he was director of their consumer and strategy consulting practices in New York and London, respectively. He has held senior strategic planning and analysis roles with Schering-Plough Pharmaceuticals and Citibank. In the early 1990s, Qaalfa worked for the city of New York and was responsible for medical, physical, and psychological occupational health standards.

He is coauthor of the book *Customer Experience Future Trends and Insights* (Palgrave Macmillan, 2010). He has been keynote speaker at a number of conferences, is frequently quoted in the international press, and has authored and published a variety of white papers and magazine and journal articles. Qaalfa is also an award-winning university professor.

He has an MBA (international business and management) from New York University and master's degrees in statistics, psychology, and health administration from the City University of New York, having graduated with departmental distinction from the State University of New York. Qaalfa is a world traveler and has lived and worked in the three of the world's great cities (New York, London, and Tokyo).

Kalina Janevska

Kalina Janevska is a business psychologist with expertise in analyzing and designing emotionally engaging customer experiences. She has experience helping companies in a variety of industries (e.g., healthcare, telecommunications, financial services, retail) and geographies (Europe, Africa, Asia) achieve cultural transformation.

Kalina has successfully designed and delivered tools and programs for employee engagement, experience assessment, journey mapping, and customer experience redesign.

Coming from a family of physicians, Kalina developed an interest in helping people better their lives at an early age.

Her curiosity to discover the root causes of people's decisions and behavior led her to study psychology and work as a teaching assistant in social psychology at the St. Cyril and Methodius University in Skopje, Macedonia, her home country. This is when she became trained in assessing and managing human psychology, interaction, and behavior.

Kalina moved to London to complete her master's degree in business psychology, which introduced her to her job as a Customer Experience consultant in Beyond Philosophy, a Customer Experience consultancy with a global footprint.

Since that time, Kalina has been the project lead on programs aimed at improving organizations' customer experiences to drive customer loyalty and greater business outcomes.

Gregory Erickson

After attending Lamar University, **Greg Erickson** joined the U.S. Navy and trained to become a nuclear medicine technologist. When his service to his country was complete, he settled in Houston, Texas, with his family. He started his postservice career as an assistant director in the Nuclear Medicine Department of Texas Children's Hospital. Due to his natural leadership abilities, he quickly moved from supervisor of a single modality to director of the Imaging Department.

In 2004, he took his talents to Community General as the director of Imaging and Cardiac Cath Labs. During the next three years, he held the unique position of leading a successful department in a struggling hospital. When the Hospital System acquired Community General some years ago, Greg quickly rose to the top at the new organization. He has been instrumental in leading the facility to a top performer in his system and community, with the facility receiving national recognition for its performance.

On a personal note, Greg has been married to his high school sweetheart for twenty years and is the father of two athletes in the making. Greg enjoys hunting, watching sports, and coaching his sons in their various sports, including football, baseball, and basketball.

The Story—What Really Happened ...

Rhonda

I walked into Community General, my community hospital, full of my normal enthusiasm and optimism. After twenty years of working in a hospital system, I had taken a position at the newest hospital acquisition. We had acquired a stand-alone hospital that was about five miles from my home. I was to be the director of Customer Experience Design and part of the transition team. Since this hospital had struggled for many years, I just knew the personnel would be thrilled to see me. I was here to save the day. I was coming from a very good and well-respected system. I knew there would be a lot of gratitude for the opportunity to become part of such an awesome company.

Greg

After two years as imaging director at Community General, the stand-alone facility was acquired by a large system. I was doing a fine job and was proud of it. I had received many accolades for heading the only department that met every financial expectation set. It was not always easy to cut staff, but I knew I had to do whatever it took to survive. I was tough. After all, at my previous hospital I had earned the title of "the Hammer" when I had to fire all seven managers under me for not performing. I had a plaque on my wall to prove it.

Chapter 1

Begin to Spark

Qaalfa: Patient Experience equals Customer Experience in a healthcare setting.
Kalina: Be clear on what Patient Experience is **not**.

At the beginning, we would like to clarify and define what Patient Experience means. It is important to understand the meaning of Patient Experience as the definition of it will affect and shape the approach and perspective you put on how your organization delivers its services and runs its operations. Drawing on knowledge about Customer Experience, the following definition applies:

> Customer Experience is best defined as *an interaction between an organization and a customer as perceived through a customer's conscious and subconscious mind. It is a blend of an organization's rational performance, the senses stimulated and the emotions evoked and intuitively measured against customer expectations across all moments of contact.*[*]

In the hospital setting, we tend to talk about the Patient Experience as the literal experience of the patient. Technically, we use Customer Experience to refer to the experience of the patient, family, friends, and visitors. However, for the remainder of this book, we use the terms *Patient Experience* and *Customer Experience* interchangeably.

---

[*] Colin Shaw and John Ivens, 2004, *Building Great Customer Experiences*, Palgrave Macmillan, Houndmills, UK.

While Patient Experience is the term most often used in hospital administration, literature, and recent legislation, Customer Experience is the term preferred by the wider business community.

As you are no doubt well aware, attempting to build a patient-centric culture will encounter resistance, especially at the start of the change. That is not a problem by itself. It is natural that the unknown creates more anxiety than excitement for the majority of workers. The difficulty comes when resistance is bolstered by a foundation of misconceptions about patient centricity that, unless openly addressed, can easily prevent successful implementation of any program. If the culture accepts these misconceptions as truths, change is unlikely to happen.

Perhaps the three most common types of fallacious ideas that undermine a patient-centric cultural shift are as follows:

1. **Fallacy 1: Customer centricity is another project we need to deliver.** This implies three things: (1) It is additional work and a burden for employees to carry out. (2) Someone else will drive it, and the individual employee just needs to know only those bits and pieces that he or she will directly execute as instructed. (3) The project will end at some point. For many, this third point is code for "let's wait this one out."
   - **Point 1:** Being patient-centric is less about doing more work (unless the work that is currently done is grossly negligent) and more about doing the same work differently. Patient Experience is a mindset that translates into a culture. The key is to get individuals to see that they need a new mindset. This mindset will help ensure that whatever projects might be necessary will be carried out in the correct spirit. Checking in a patient can be done in a transactional manner and quickly, or it can be done quickly and with care. In the second instance, it is the same activity but executed with the intent of showing care. Projects carried out without this mindset (without the correct spirit) are most often "tick-box" exercises at best. These rarely produce the desired sustained effects in Patient Experience terms. Care can be shown in many ways, but when genuine, it is easily recognized by patients.
   - **Point 2:** Patient centricity has to be thought of as ether rather than a pill. It needs to be in the air. There will always be pressure to deliver it in pill form but resist if you are not delivering those pills while infusing the organization with the ether. Projects are equivalent to pills. Education and coaching are more akin to the ether.
   - **Point 3:** It has often been said that Customer Experience is a journey, not a destination. As such, you will always be headed toward the horizon. You will pass landmarks along the way, but these are simply milestones marking the organization's evolution. Creating the Customer Experience mindset by infusing the environment with the ether will enable the organization to keep its eye on the horizon and appreciate the milestones along the journey.

2. **Fallacy 2: Customer centricity is something concerning only those who give care directly (i.e., customer-facing employees).** This is one of the most widely accepted misconceptions about patient centricity. With the way HCAHPS (Hospital Consumer Assessment of Healthcare Providers and Systems) is currently structured, or most customer satisfaction surveys for that matter, managers can easily be misguided into thinking that it is those in the front line who need to improve communication and delivery. Remember from the definition of Customer Experience that the most basic understanding of Patient Experience is that it is the interaction between the *whole organization* and the patient. Done correctly, it should be apparent that releasing the Customer Experience ether will (and should) affect everyone at the hospital. This is a profound point and should not be overlooked. For all intents and purposes, any approach that focuses resources solely on training customer-facing employees and neglects those who play their roles behind the scenes is wasting money and time. Sooner or later, mostly sooner, decisions made somewhere higher up in the hierarchy or in the non-patient-facing departments will affect those customer-facing employees' ability to deliver a great Patient Experience. Moreover, non-patient-facing departments often create touch points with which patients do interact. Examples include the medical bill, hospital Web site, signage to the premises, or tidiness of the cleaning staff and uniforms. All of these touch points help determine the patients' perception of the experience. The point is that all employees and departments need the same grounding in Patient Experience. Customer Experience is a way of running your business and organization, not just a tool.

3. **Fallacy 3: Customer centricity is about being better at what we are already doing.** This is a bit more subtle than the others but no less a fallacy. This idea is usually expressed as: "We need to be more efficient in doing what we do because that would allow us to do more of it." Those who propose this put emphasis on the words *better* or *more efficient*. Unfortunately, what happens in the real world is that unenlightened managers and employees focus on the concept of what they "are already doing." Of course, if current practices do not deliver the results you seek, more of the current practice is unlikely to do so. The fallacy is that people will often think: "Basically, we are already doing Patient Experience. Of course, we can improve, but we are already doing it." The implicit outcome of that sort of thinking is that employees then think that Customer Experience is about doing things more frequently or speedily or with greater precision when, in fact, it is more about having a predefined intent that is expressed through the interaction, regardless of what the interaction is. This intent is usually what is missing, and too often employees rely on activities and tasks and their volume, frequency, or precision.

It would be ideal if there ware a silver bullet or a list of twenty sure-fire things you need to do to achieve Patient Experience excellence. Best practice exists, but a best practice implemented in an unenlightened way is just a tick-box exercise. Tick-box exercises can produce momentary bumps in performance, but these are generally not sustainable. What is required is a culture that allows staff decision making and work to evolve together with patients' needs and perceptions. An established Patient Experience culture is essentially an inextinguishable source of initiatives that lead to excellence.

Rhonda: This is not what I expected!

When I walked into my office, which was still being used for gift shop storage and had no office furniture or equipment, my optimism was a bit shaken. It was like they forgot I was coming. My space was full of boxes, and I did not even have a chair to sit in. I quickly began to wonder how happy they were to have me join their team. My first interaction with a fellow leader sealed the deal on those feelings. As she peered at me over her glasses and snarled, "Just what makes you think you are qualified to come into this hospital?" I started to question my decision to come to this place. After all, I left a job in the system where I was well respected for the outcomes I had delivered. A few more interactions when I was told, "Do not expect me to drink your Kool-Aid," and was referred to as "hon" in a not-so-endearing way sent me back to my chair in the hallway to devise a plan. I had been given a chair in a hallway to work from while they removed the crystal from my office space. I was determined, more than determined really, to make a difference in the transition of the hospital. This hospital was less than four miles from my parents' home. I needed to feel it was a great place in case they needed it. I first had to find my allies in this transformation journey, so I decided to meet with all of the leadership individually to get an idea of where everyone stood. This led me to the office of "the Hammer." I was meeting with Gregory Erickson, the director of Imaging Services. I could not help but wonder who the heck would want to be known as the Hammer. As I was shown to his office door, the first thing I noticed was a plaque on the wall with a literal hammer attached to it. A brass plate was inscribed with, "Gregory Erickson, Radiology Administration," and "The Hammer." Again, I asked myself, what have I gotten into?

Greg: Whatever—my numbers are great.

This new system was coming in, and there was a change and a new idea for every minute of the day. Were these people crazy? Before they came in, it was a pretty relaxing place to work. Nowadays, it was jumping through hoops just to respond to all of the training needs for all of the new ways of doing things. My staff did not even know how to clock in anymore. I looked at my calendar and braced myself for my meeting with the newest member of this acquisition team. They had brought in a new director of Customer Experience Design. It was not that I was not supportive of that customer satisfaction stuff, but quite frankly, who had the time right now? It did not matter what I did anyway. I knew how it worked. Whenever a stand-alone hospital is bought out by a large system, they fire all of the directors and bring in their own or new ones. My resumé had been brushed up and was in the mail. For now, however, I had to keep the appointment.

After the meeting, I reflected that these were some great ideas, and I could get somewhat inspired. We talked about seeing things from a patient's perspective. I could easily see where we could do that and the impact it would have. I could be inspired if I could see the forest for the trees. There was continual turmoil with all of the change. I was a numbers guy by nature, so I pulled productivity reports daily. I could tell you every free minute for every one of my employees. I also could account for every Band-Aid bought, needle used, and test charged for. This new director, Rhonda, was talking numbers, but they were numbers I had never seen before. They were numbers around patient satisfaction. There was an "n," a mean score and a percentile ranking. She kept talking about us being in the first percentile and comparing that to being at the bottom of your graduating class. She said that your mean score is like your grade point average, but your percentile was where you fell among your peers. So, if you are in the first percentile, ninety-nine percent of your peers are outscoring you. She went on to explain how to pull the numbers and where they came from. I liked what she was saying, but I was not sure I was up for the challenge of all of this change. I went home and sent some more resumés.

Rhonda: See the spark.

After my meeting with the Hammer, I was somewhat inspired. Although he seemed far from engaged, I did see a tiny spark. It only takes a spark, and it was the only one I had seen outside of the administration suite. He definitely understood numbers and reports. In fact, he probably could teach me something about reading reports and numbers. I could tell that he was inspired by a challenge and was competitive by nature. Other than the hammer plaque, his office was filled with photographs of a young boy in various sporting outfits. He also had several photos and plaques indicating he was a "coach." If he could coach kids to play ball, he could coach employees to create and deliver experiences. I knew this was a guy I needed to get on my side. As I watched him interact with other leaders during the next few weeks, I could see he was well respected. I definitely needed to get him aligned.

It was evident immediately that the only way to move this hospital would be a complete culture overhaul. It would not be just a sprucing up but a complete change. I started pulling out all of my old material and researching new material around culture change and how it is best done. I had much success at this on a departmental level, but I was afraid I had undertaken more than I could accomplish. Maybe I needed to brush up my resumé. In the meantime, however, I was determined to try.

A few months later, I got a call from the Hammer. This confident leader with the most success in the building up until now called for help. I was afraid I would not be good enough to offer the help he needed. I kept thinking of that boy in the baseball outfit and knew a family was depending on my ability. I had just had my yearly evaluation that morning and had been praised for my ability to inspire and teach. If any of it was true, I would need it all now. There were many of us that had different abilities. The trick would be to pull all of our talent together to make this happen. Not only was a community depending on this place to turn around, but real families of the employees were, too, including mine!

Greg: Reality check.

I went to my COO's [chief operating officer's] office for my annual evaluation. I knew what to expect because I had always received great evaluations. After all, I was the department not losing money. As soon as I was greeted by him, I could tell this one would be different. He did not begin with fluff compliments; he went straight for the jugular. His first point was that my employee satisfaction was the second worst in the hospital, or was it system? Next, he attacked my patient satisfaction, letting me know 98% of imaging departments across the country were outperforming mine. He also mentioned the physicians did not particularly like working with me or my department. I kept waiting for the good stuff. The other shoe to drop, you know? The forgiveness for all of this because I was making money for this place! The forgiveness never came. He explained that we worry about quality and satisfaction first and let finances come after. I did not know what to do with this new perspective. I knew they had talked about all of this other stuff, but I did not know it was this real. I expected money to outweigh all of the bad. I left not knowing how to take being given twelve months to turn it all around. I did not even know where to start. I had to have the help of someone who understood all of this "nice" stuff. I called Rhonda.

Rhonda: Fan that spark.

This was the beginning of two opposites joining forces, balancing strengths with weaknesses, and surviving together. It started with the two of us but involved an entire team working together. I met with Greg, and we discussed the challenges that we were both experiencing. I knew this was going to be different. He was not afraid to tell me when I was wrong, but also was not afraid to ask for opinions when he was not sure if he was right. We knew it was not going to be easy; we understood it was going to take a complete culture overhaul, but we knew we could be a good force to reckon with together. We would not do it alone, but at the beginning, we felt very alone.

Chapter 2

Personalize to Motivate

Introduction

The real challenge was how to motivate 1,000 people in the cause to improve Patient Experience. How do you make this cause their cause? The only way was to eat the elephant one bite at a time. Rhonda and now Greg knew they would get nowhere in this culture change without motivation of the masses. There were still many mixed emotions about the transition from being a stand-alone hospital that seemed to have been swallowed up by the big guy to becoming a member of that very large system. The problem facing them was compounded by the fact that there was a huge amount of animosity from many of the employees at the takeover. It was crucial to motivate the employees so they would become willing participants in the culture change.

The Story: What Really Happened …

Rhonda: Self-reflection first.

Now that Greg and I were allies in this journey, we were looking for action. Action of some sort often happens on its own, but when left to chance, this action takes its own direction. Deliberate action pointed in the right direction takes motivation. The problem was motivation is a very personal thing. Our first step was to understand motivation. It was obvious that motivation is different for each of us. Even the two of us had been motivated by completely opposite drivers for wanting to succeed with Patient Experience as a program of action. While Greg, "the Hammer," was initially motivated by fear for his job, I, "the Pollyanna," was motivated by providing care for the community where my parents lived. At least those were the reasons on the surface. First, we had to do some self-reflection on whether all of this effort would really be worth it. Face it, my parents had been getting healthcare for years by driving a little further up the freeway, and this was not the only position in town for a director of imaging with proven results in the financial arena. We parted ways that afternoon still in joint forces but knowing this would not be easy, so we would really have to be all in.

Greg: Make it personal.

I went home and tried to decide what to do. I had just about talked myself into starting a new job search when my motivation came to me. When I was sixteen years old, my dad took me to an auction to buy my first car. I was so excited. I had arrived! I was going to have my own car. The next morning, my brother woke me before he went to work to ask me about my new car. While we were talking, we heard my dad's alarm sound. We chuckled because we knew he would not get up, and we would hear it for a while. My dad always set his alarm but never got up by it. My brother left for work, and I went back to sleep. Next thing I knew, I was being awakened by my panicking mom telling me something was wrong with my dad. I rushed to the bathroom, where I found him on the floor with his eyes rolled back in his head. His breathing was definitely off. He would not breathe for a period of time and then suddenly his body would shudder with a breath. I had never formally learned CPR but had seen it on TV. I knew I had to do something, so I started doing CPR the way I thought it was done. My mom ran across the street to my uncle's house to get help. Once my uncle arrived, he called 911. I had been "working" on my dad this whole time. When the ambulance arrived, the paramedics took over. After a few minutes, they put him on a stretcher and put him in the ambulance. I peeked into the window of the ambulance. I could see on the monitor that there were lines. I did not know how to read a monitor, but I knew the lines were not straight or flat, so I breathed a sigh of relief that my dad was going to be okay.

As my family and I entered the doors of the hospital, we were met by some of the staff. Right there in the middle of that hospital corridor, I learned that my dad had been pronounced dead upon arrival at the hospital. We spent a minute with his body, saying good-bye. My grandparents arrived; we had to go get my brother; people had to be called, and everything became a bit of a blur. I was too young to realize how that morning would shape my entire future. I went forward with my life. I graduated high school, got married, went to college, joined the U.S. Navy, and started a family. My choices were always guided by my father's influence. My career choices were especially peppered by the experience of my father's death. Being the first person to find my dad and to respond to the emergency infused in me a need to impact the health of others; therefore, I chose a job in healthcare.

I was determined to touch people in these vulnerable times and to make it easy to get the care they need. People will be more compliant when it is easy. Suddenly, I had no mixed feelings about taking on this challenge. I knew I had to do this, and I had to do it here.

Rhonda: Make it personal.

On a cold January morning, my grandmother was brought to the emergency center of the hospital where I had worked for the past fifteen years. I was very proud of where I worked and defiantly defended the hospital any time anyone questioned healthcare in general. You are probably familiar with the snide comments about a ten-dollar Tylenol and such. What people did not realize is the number of people that abuse hospitals. There are many people who ignore their condition until it is too late or that run to the ED [emergency department] rather than going to a doctor's office. We were there day in and day out, saving lives and providing care. How dare they question the costs associated with such important work or that we did not always have time to be nice. So, here I was on the other side of the desk. This was my beloved grandmother lying on that stretcher. One of the most important people in my life was sick and scared, and that scared me more than I wanted to admit.

For the next sixteen days, we were patients in my hospital. In what seemed like minutes, things were going in the wrong direction. Grandma was not getting better; she was worse. We found ourselves in ICU [intensive care unit] with little knowledge as to what was causing her to be sick. After a very long and frustrating three days, we found ourselves in a room being told that she was not going to pull through. This was the same person we had spent Christmas with less than a month earlier. This was the same person who was asking me to bring her breakfast a week earlier. This was my grandma. There were thirty-two years of memories connected to that hospital bed. Even more difficult than watching my grandmother was watching my mother go through this. The night my grandmother died did not find my family surrounded by loving people who were supporting us as the time ticked away. Instead, we found hospital personnel who became frustrated with our fears and relentless efforts to not let her go. As we waited for the end, we overheard a nurse complaining to her peers about all of the visitors in my grandmother's room. She exclaimed that she wished this had happened on the day shift so she would not have to deal with us. I was no longer her coworker; now, I was her problem.

There were high points as well. The security officer who came and took my grandmother's body away gave my hand a squeeze as he passed by. The doctor expressed sincere grief in not being able to save her. The previous week, our hospital had begun tracking patient satisfaction. In a mandatory session, I had listened as the speaker talked about treating every patient well during every interaction. This had really intrigued me, but now that I was a part of the patient class and not just the employee class, it really made sense. The night my grandmother died, I whispered to her to rest easy and vowed that I would dedicate my career to doing everything possible to make sure no other family ever had negative interactions laced in their memories of their precious family member's death. The next time I was at work, I went to Administration and asked how I could join the team working on patient satisfaction. That was ten years before. I had worked throughout this system to make a difference for the patients and their family members. It was that motivation that I channeled again. It was that promise to Grandma that would give me the strength to make this happen.

Now that we were fully engaged and had rekindled our reasons for being in our field, we knew we had to find a way to get others to join our cause. We talked endlessly about making this happen. We read all of the books of ideas to implement. We knew, though, that none of those would work until we had a culture in which they could thrive.

Greg had been an expert on motivating by fear. Although that had worked to achieve success on a singular strategy level, he knew that it would not be enough to achieve this complete transformation. He had been shocked into action by the fear of losing his job, but that fear was no longer his motivation. I had been an expert on motivating people by making it fun and for overrewarding them for every little thing. Those types of motivation have short-term effects. Long-term motivation, the kind we needed, came from value alignment.

Greg told me that you motivate one person at a time. Since we are all individuals, motivation has to be personal. That does not mean it has to occur one on one. The message can be given to groups, but everyone has to hear it and be able to personalize it to move them to action. Since I did not have a vast line of direct reports as the director of Patient Experience, I started spending a lot of time with the staff that reported to other leaders. I believed strongly that success was an attitude with a lot of work behind it. The work would get you nowhere without the attitude and vice versa. In essence, you need to walk the talk and talk the walk. When I rounded on the staff in the various departments, I talked about us as though we were already the best of the best. When I spoke of our mission and values, it was very matter of fact. It was just the way we do things. I could see the light go on for many of the people I was talking to. People were getting excited. They were still very cautious, but the spark was lit.

There were others who did not get motivated by the message. I was patient, though. Many of them were just like Greg. They had become a product of their environment and had been in survival mode for so long it would not be an easy transition into success mode. The thing about motivation is you can offer inspiration; you can tell the story and spread the message, but ultimately, they have to choose to be motivated. Just like Greg and I had to reach deep inside for our reasons to make this worth it, they would as well. What I soon learned is there was a large group of people who were not going to be able to do that. They were not bad people. I watched a lot of very nice people, people I had learned to care a lot about, walk out the door for the last time. Although it made me sad, the success of the whole was more important than any of us as individuals. If they did not have it in them, for whatever reason, they belonged outside. It was hard, but I had to accept it. I had to reach those that I could. I had to reach them early on. Where could I tell the story from the earliest point? I needed to find a way to plant the seed early on, set the expectation.

Greg: Balancing carrot and stick.

I realized that motivation begins inside each of us as individuals. Just as I had to summon my original reasons for serving in health-care, each of the people on this team would have to find their own personal reason for making the necessary changes. I had motivated the team in my department with the hammer for so long, I was not sure I would be credible with any other method. Besides, I was not sure I knew how to motivate in any other way. Hammering had worked for efficiency and productivity, but employee, patient, and physician satisfaction took a more personal contribution of effort. It required an emotional transference and not just a transactional one. I needed to find someone for that balance. I had been interviewing candidates for the manager of my department. I had who I would have previously thought to be the perfect candidate. She was just like me. She would reinforce my hammer with her own. Now, however, I was starting to think I needed someone different. Perhaps I needed someone who was good at recognizing and having fun. I had interviewed another candidate who fit that description. She had a great attitude, and service and recognition seemed intuitive to her, but she had absolutely no leadership experience. This would be a big gamble, a bigger gamble than I was used to making. I called her and made the offer. I pushed down the fear this caused and took a chance on something completely different.

I began to spread the message in every possible opportunity to my team through the new manager. This allowed me to ease into a different communication style. I knew I still could not accept anything less than close-to-perfect performance, I just had to motivate for those results in a different manner. Rewarding for small steps of success was the first order of business. Rhonda thanked people for the smallest efforts, and when I questioned her, she told me that if you want someone to keep doing something, even small things, let them know you like it. It seemed like a waste of compliments at first, but I soon found that it worked. This team that I had hammered into submission was being rewarded into success on all of our strategies. I kept the hammer ready for when it was needed, but I knew after they were shocked into immediate compliance, long-term performance could be attained through aligning with what was important to them. Just as I connected my mission to making preventive care available and easy as an honor to my dad, they had all been drawn into this career for personal reasons as well. They may not all have a reason such as mine, but putting food on the table for your family is just as honorable a cause. In no time at all, my team was responding to my new way of inspiring. Honestly, I liked it better, too.

Although people were excited and were beginning to focus on creating exceptional customer experiences, the sparks were not spreading like wildfire in all areas. I had to make these concepts real to everyone on my team. Unlike our previous culture, the new system had a pay-for-performance evaluation process. Sixty percent of an individual's evaluation, and therefore raise, was directly tied to his or her performance around ten goals. I had recently learned the reality of that in my evaluation. Timing was perfect. We were just setting goals for the next year. I had previously set all of the goals around productivity. The goals would now be divided up among all of the strategies. I needed to call my team together to make these new goals their idea so they would buy in. Measuring our outcomes and the behaviors that determined them was the glue that I needed to make this new culture stick. What I was not fully aware of at that time was that everyone on my team would not be up for this challenge. Some of them would not even want this new way of thinking. I had to balance carefully my new way of thinking and motivating, but at the same time I had to keep accountability in the center of all of this. I could not be afraid to lose a tech that was good at his imaging skills but bad at these newly required skills. Just as my boss was not afraid to have a difficult conversation with me filled with consequences, I would have to do the same with my team.

Rhonda: Motivate sideways, too.

As I rounded on the different departments, it soon became evident that not all of the leadership and employees were aligned with the changes in our culture. Perhaps they were just tired from so many attempts and the sometimes-overwhelming amount of work it would take. There was a large group of our employees who were on board with the changes in culture. They were high performers by nature and were quickly becoming frustrated. That is the way with high performers when they are aligned with something: They can be unstoppable. They are the power you need to get the wheels in motion. If they are not being led by a leader who shares their mission or has the abilities to have the tough conversations with those not onboard, they are a flight risk. If they do not see the ability to succeed because the leaders they depend on are in their way, they will seek a team with which they can succeed.

Greg shared the same frustrations that I was feeling. His department worked closely with the other departments in the hospital. Imaging worked with every other area—emergency, the nursing floors, even registration. Greg was working hard and making a lot of progress with his team, but they were getting frustrated when they saw their work on Patient Experience being undone once the patient left their department. Greg was hitting a lot of road blocks when he talked to those other departmental leaders. Now, Greg and I felt ourselves in a position with not only a responsibility to provide healthcare for our community but also to provide an environment where success was possible for these members of our team. Our focus now expanded from motivation of the front line to include motivation of the midlevel leadership team as well. It was time to call for reinforcements. There was a suite of chiefs who had proven over and over that they expected success and a focus on creating this culture to serve our community. Considering the power in numbers and the power in their positions, we headed to Administration to gain buy-in, explain the implications and get them to join the cause in earnest.

The Lesson: What You Need to Know ...

Qaalfa: Invest in carrots but have stick insurance.
Kalina: See the experience as your patients do.

All too often, transformation programs within organizations start, and end, with the big launch—uncorking the proverbial champagne, posters visible on every wall, and a grand hall presentation to the employees. However, successful transformation often starts with a small group of people, much discussion, and subtle but important changes that build over time and spread unobtrusively. Rhonda and Greg were the sole igniters of Patient Experience when they were faced with the challenge to improve their hospital's patient satisfaction results. Rhonda was the flint, Greg the first spark. They had passion and determination—the key ingredients necessary in creating a reliable force of pioneers.

It is no surprise that motivating employees will not happen at once, as any motivation or management book will attest. In fact, it will start very small, with a few people who will have doubts and questions at the beginning. As they learn, their confidence will grow, their enthusiasm will rub off onto colleagues, and those colleagues will spread it to others and so on.

But, how do you initiate that interest? Rhonda and Greg answered this question beautifully. As a first step, due to unfortunate personal circumstances, they walked the experience their patients walk every day. Even though they had been walking the same halls and talking to the same people every day at work, they had done so with their professional hats on, as employees and part of the organization. This was even true for Rhonda, although she was a true blue believer in Patient Experience and a skilled practitioner by the time she got to Community General. It was not until her loving grandmother was admitted that she truly began to "see" the experience.

Viewing the same halls as actual patients do made all the difference to her motivation because now she felt the significance of it. Suddenly, all the little things that make up that experience, that were more or less invisible before, became important and noteworthy. She realized the value their work has in someone else's life, their patient's life.

The process of the experience does not equate to the story of the experience. The story of the experience is not made up only of the major characters, plot, theme, and setting; it is also the choice of words, paragraph length, font size, page color, narration style, and so on. When Rhonda and Greg viewed the experience from the outside-in with a personal lens, they immediately changed their perspective and perception of what was in fact happening in their hospital and how that had an impact on patients' lives. All the subtle clues that impressed on their experience, their expectations, their fears, and their hopes had reshaped the way they assessed reality in the hospital. This could never be conveyed in feedback surveys from customers, and even if it was, it could not touch them as deeply as experiencing it did.

Of course, not everyone has had so personal an experience with hospitals, but that does not preclude them from understanding the hospital experience from an outside-in perspective. In a nutshell, what the field of Customer Experience is about is getting employees at all levels to be able to see the experience from the customer's point of view. In fact, there are many techniques and tools you can use to get your staff to see the experience patients have, focusing purposefully on picking up the subtle clues that convey the sense of care, comfort, or whatever it is the hospital intends to convey.

In the simplest form, seeing the experience from a patients' perspective is essentially an honest introspective reflection on previous experiences you would have had as a patient or a customer. In the more typical case, it involves coaching employees through a structured system of taking in the end-to-end emotional and psychological experience from the point of view of the patient. It opens employees' eyes about the actual experience of the patients and in so doing gets them to see how elements of the environment or interaction have an impact on that particular patient journey, especially the little things that are often overlooked. More important, they understand the significance of that experience (rational and emotional) to the customer as a human being. Once this basic understanding is there, it may take a bit more coaching for those "aha moments" to take hold. An aha moment is when an employee says, "I get it now; I see what this is really all about." That is the moment when you are closest to being able to tap into their internal motivation and when genuine care and passion is born.

Since different employees respond differently, the organization will need to approach motivation systematically and from different angles. For those who can easily see the experience as patients do and feel inspired by it, informal methods will work well and give results from the beginning. For employees who find it difficult to appreciate the importance of the experience, formal methods will be required at the beginning.

Formal methods are those that are sanctioned by the institution, and the motivation they produce is extrinsic in nature.

Some forms may sound familiar to strategy-oriented managers. Some organizations may have already implemented these:

- Define the intended Patient Experience and clearly communicate it within the organization.
- Make Patient Experience objectives part of business objectives in the official hospital strategy.
- Include Patient Experience as part of the staff's personal objectives.
- Include Patient Experience measures as part of the bonus/remuneration system for staff.
- Include Patient Experience objectives in business case templates.

The point here is that the hospital clearly and officially commits to making Patient Experience excellence a key strategic goal and makes it known to staff that it is serious about it.

The hospital system had more than twenty years of focus and success in patient satisfaction. Community General had that experience as a foundation. There were several challenges unique to this facility that required more trial and error and persistence. Rhonda and Greg not only led the efforts for their departments but also influenced the hospital as a whole. They did this as part of a team but were often the leaders of the efforts. When departmental and personal objectives related to performance-based rewards are affected, it is serious. Greg's subordinates understood this for they had to face the Hammer if they were performing less than optimally on key metrics.

Extrinsic motivation, however, does not produce a lasting effect when practiced in isolation. In fact, in the beginning, when many employees are not yet displaying the desired behaviors and just starting to learn what it means to behave in a customer-centric way, these formal methods are likely to be experienced by them as more punishing (i.e., "stick") rather than rewarding (i.e., "carrot"). In time, as employees become engaged and intrinsically motivated, they will begin to see these as a support system and enabler of their culture. Be aware that this second step is not guaranteed, and many organizations continue their formal methods without the desired results. Under such circumstances, if the threat of punishment is lessened or removed (e.g., when a manager leaves), undesired behavior will likely increase in frequency, and customer-centric behavior will be extinguished.

Extrinsic motivation can be easy to install, but it is also relatively easy to dissipate. Extrinsic motivation via the hammer on its own requires constant vigilance and generally creates a harsh, negative atmosphere, a sense of employees being pressured, which is at odds with what Patient Experience is trying to achieve.

Informal methods, on the other hand, feel personal and rely heavily on carrot. We use the term *carrot* here to describe an approach based on giving something valuable to employees that is meaningful to them at a personal and individual level. The goal is to tie in to employees' intrinsic motivation. In time, carrots (i.e., rewards) rely on peer pressure—feeding on people's desire to fit in with their respected coworkers. Informal methods are generally learned and promulgated through observation, coaching, and one-to-one interactions. As a result, it may take a longer time frame for informal methods to take hold. However, it also takes more time for these effects of informal methods to expire. The informal way is generally more sustainable than a formal approach. It is well known that intrinsic motivation is more effective than extrinsic motivation. Intrinsic motivation is akin to cultural transformation. We address informal ways of motivation in Chapter 6, "Succeed, then Recognize." For now, it is important to understand the difference between the two approaches. Of course, it is necessary to have both in your arsenal.

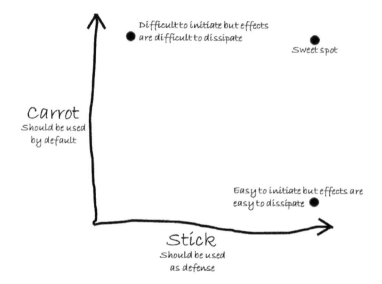

The informal carrot-friendly approach is central to sustainable cultural transformation. This is the equivalent of Rhonda's natural style, and it is what Greg sought in his right-hand manager. Essentially, Greg came to understand that he needed the carrot as much as he needed the stick. In fact, he learned it is better to use the carrot by default. However, both Greg and Rhonda understood that the stick is required if an employee cannot or will not come into the Customer Experience fold.

Understanding, addressing, and tapping into employees' motivation is central to becoming an effective change manager. Let us be clear: Addressing motivation is *not* about becoming a "happy-clappy" manager with great intentions and no guts. Greg said it best: "This team that I had hammered into submission was being rewarded into success on all of our strategies. I kept the hammer ready for when it was needed, but I knew after they were shocked into immediate compliance long-term performance could be attained through aligning with what was important to them."

The following are key steps to motivating:

- Walk your patients' experience to understand the emotional experience, the subtle clues, the little things, and the psychological journey your patients have.
- Use informal methods of motivation to tap into employees' intrinsic reward systems.
- Do as much as you can to make Patient Experience excellence a formal objective, whether through incorporating it in personal objectives, the formal reward system, or the official hospital strategy. This will allow you to pull out your hammer on the potentially rare occasions when you need to.
- Motivate across the organization, not just customer-facing staff.

Chapter 3

Serve to Lead

The Story: What Really Happened ...

Greg: Service trumps rank.

I learned a lot of my leadership style as a subordinate during my service in the Navy. It was kind of like they owned us. Rank equaled respect. If you were a lower rank, you obeyed orders, no questions asked. Again, I was young, and I acted on the value of not getting into trouble. So, if they outranked me and they said do it, I did it. Because this was my last experience with leadership before I started my career as a civilian, this was the mentality I took with me. When I received my first position in management, I knew failure was not an option. I drilled results out of my staff. If there was a number we had to reach I would not rest until they reached it. To my thinking, I had the rank and therefore was due the respect. Wow, what an eye opener the first time an employee quit because he did not like my management style. I did not let that stand in my way, though. If they wanted to leave, there were plenty more out there to replace them—and until they were hired and trained, the rest of the staff would just have to work harder.

My very first experience with leadership was while playing sports as a kid. One thing that quickly became apparent upon reflection was that leadership does not necessarily come with a title, and those who have the titles are not automatically leaders. In whatever sport I was a part of, I found myself being looked to for answers and direction from my teammates. I was never the "captain of the football team," but I was always the one guiding the others. Of course, I was not fully aware of the reasons at the time, but as I look back, I know that the reason my peers put me in that role was service. I was willing to do anything for my team. I did not look down at the other players. In fact, I instinctively knew that the team would only be as good as the weakest player. If I saw one of the other guys struggling, I was there to offer assistance. I was not in it for my own glory but for that of the team. No job was too big or too small for me. If it needed to be done, I was the first one in, whether it was grunge work or accepting the awards.

My military-taught style had worked fine for me until that fateful day when the CEO [chief executive officer] informed me that money is not the only thing that counts, and not even the most important thing. Now that retention and employee satisfaction were on par with operational excellence, I had to reach back to those sporting days and link back to my original style of leadership. So, I began to rely less on my rank and more on my service to those around me. I expected them to give it all for the team's success, but I was right there with them leading them to the victory.

Rhonda: Serve to lead.

When I was a little kid, I thought of power kind of like that cartoon *Pinky and the Brain*, about two white lab rats who wanted to take over the world. There was The Brain, the "smart" rat, always plotting to be the leader. He was careful not to hang around with anyone he considered his equal because he did not want to be challenged for the position of dictator. Therefore, he was left to have only one rather dense "rat" follower to help him with his plots. Of course, every episode ended with the takeover plot failing and the world left to conquer. I did not get it, though; I still thought leaders are dictators and in charge. The bosses are the ones that get to come in late, tell everyone what to do, and go home early, right? I was the president of several organizations in high school. Of course, those organizations had responsibilities. Fulfilling responsibilities requires a volunteer workforce. Volunteers do not have to show up, and they do not have to do it right.

In one of my classes in high school, I was taught to put sets together for the school plays. The teacher who showed us how to make the sets was relentless. She yelled her demands and publicly scolded if we did not do it right. Later in the year, I was responsible for getting the sets put together for our first performance. As per her example, I was prepared to stand back and watch as the "team" put them together. Well, much to my surprise, only two people showed up when the task required at least ten. I had not counted on the fact that in the classroom there was a grade at stake; here, there was simply the reward of participating. I reacted to the stress of not having enough laborers by barking orders at the two workers who were there to help. It never crossed my mind that I should be helping with the task. After all, the teacher had never helped us in class; she simply yelled until she got what she wanted. It did not take long before the volunteers left, and I was not only needed to help, but to do it all on my own! There was a very strict deadline, so I worked through the night on those sets. I learned where the buck stops. If you want to get it done and no one else shows, the leaders get to do the work.

On my next opportunity to lead a group, which was heading up the school's food drive, I was very gracious and included all of the team's opinions in the plan for the day. I let them know how important our mission was and made them feel good about the job they were about to do. I also led by example. I did not ask them to do anything I was not willing to do as well. I also learned to serve the team. If I saw that they needed something, I got it for them. Not only did no one walk off from that assignment, but also they worked to recruit more help. Together, we had the most successful drive in the history of the school. When the local paper came to take our picture, I made sure I was in the back and the quotes in the article came from other members of the team. That really formed my leadership style. What I learned in that experience is that I am more comfortable as a servant leader than as the dictator. I get fulfillment from giving. Sorry, Pinky; you and The Brain are not going to take over the world today: We are going to serve the team that leads the mission.

Growing up, my parents believed strongly in community involvement. They served in the parent-teacher organization, youth organizations, and church. I thought it was just a way of life. I grew up with little money of our own, but I remember every holiday season collecting toys and food for those who were less fortunate. The satisfaction of serving others was instilled in me at a very early age. What I did not learn well was that balance. I was a giver and a leader, but I had to learn the dangers of entitlement. When you give to someone without expecting anything back or teaching them the satisfaction of earning it, you are not being fair to them. I learned a lot about how to do that through conversations with Greg. Funny how I thought I was coming in to teach the leaders of our newly acquired hospital, but this one taught me so much more.

Greg and I spent a lot of time talking about leadership and service. We were continually challenged and even perplexed by the department-level leaders on our hospital team. Our CEO was the perfect example of a servant leader. During my interview for my role as a director on his team, I noticed an antique clay water pitcher on his desk. My curiosity got the best of me, and I asked him about it. He thought for a moment and explained it was there to remind him that he is here to serve. It was then that I decided I wanted this job. I had been familiar with this CEO when he was in a different role in the system. There were a lot of reasons I had accepted this opportunity to interview, but going in I was still very skeptical. All doubts left when I heard his reasoning for what I thought was a decoration. After accepting the position, I knew it was not just words but the way he led. Greg and I talked about the CEO's style, and we were learning to be better leaders by his example. Sometimes, it seemed there was resistance to follow his example by some of our peers. That was one thing we never understood: How can someone see such grace, caring, and commitment from their leader and not incorporate those characteristics into their own style?

Before we started seeing success, there were some really dark days at our hospital. Leaders and employees were having difficulty adjusting to the new standards for service and quality. As measured by the system expectations, our outcomes often found us performing on the bottom. It was tough to work there during that time, but the CEO made every teardrop and drop of sweat worth the effort. I remember one day I came to work on a Sunday. I liked to round on the weekends to get the story from every perspective. I was surprised to pass the CEO and CNO [chief nursing officer] in the hallway outside of the Emergency Department [ED] pushing an empty stretcher back into the treatment area. When I asked the CEO what he was doing, he said they were working as ED techs. He had received a call from a concerned employee in the ED as he was leaving for church. They were short several nurses and had no techs scheduled for that day. He sent his family to church, called the CNO, and they came to work.

For years after that, you still heard the employees talking about the day the CEO and CNO came in to stock linens and empty trash cans. He created that kind of an environment. We all, from directors to front line, felt comfortable coming to him with anything. An ED nurse had felt at ease calling him when he found himself in trouble and without a departmental leader he was confident in. It was not an environment that welcomed tattling, though. If you came to him without first exhausting efforts with the individual in question, he sent you back. He helped in the situation and took care of the lack of engagement with the department director as well. It was learning that kind of balance from him and Greg that made me stronger. I was putting so much in every single day, but I was getting tenfold back.

Greg: True colors come out in a crisis.

Hurricanes frequent our area. It was in the response to a particularly bad one that I learned which leaders were engaged and which ones were not. In preparation for the crisis, employees and leaders were divided into teams. Team A would be the first to report to duty and would be relieved by Team B when the weather allowed. Team A strolled in to work carrying enough personal belongings to get them through a few days. The mood was one of anxiety, but there was also a sense of excitement for the adventure. The storm took over our community about midnight. There were trees blowing and rain pelting the windows. The first thing to go was phone service. Things started to escalate quickly when the hospital sign came crashing from the roof. The building began to leak, and we were soon on generator power. Overall, though, we fared well. Things were going according to the emergency plan Community General's management set out. The water supply was fine, phone lines were back up, we were well staffed, and the generators were doing their job. We were even able to serve a hot breakfast to our patients and staff.

All was well until the backup generators servicing our adult and neonatal intensive care units went down around 10 a.m., causing an evacuation of all patients on ventilators. That was the event that created a team out of a lot of individual departments. Each of the ventilated patients had to be carried down the stairs on backboards while being hand bagged,* with flashlights illuminating the path. This required coordinated effort of the carriers, the hand bagger, and the flashlight holder, all the while keeping the safety, trust, and comfort of the patient at the top of our thoughts. We succeeded.

Once those patients were all safe and accounted for, we realized that the same generator was used to keep humidity out of the operating rooms. We would lose lots of supplies if we did not act pretty quickly. We had to put all hands on deck clearing the supplies and moving them to a safe area. Many of those hands were already pretty tired. Everyone pulled together and participated; there were system and hospital senior leadership working next to the employees from housekeeping and facilities. There were potentially a lot of dollars that would go to waste if we did not clear the supplies quickly. Those dollars were an afterthought, though. We went into that area with the mission of ensuring we had the supplies needed if one of our patients were to need surgery. That was telling of our character. It had already become strong in our culture to put safety first and then consider cost. We had rescued the people needing us, and now it was time to save the supplies.

These efforts identified the people that were to make up our new culture.

Rhonda: We know you care.

We found ourselves facing the challenge of a big, direct hit hurricane. By this time, we had a leadership team made up of individuals that had a history of success at other hospitals inside and outside of our system. These were proven people by every traditional measure of success. Unfortunately, the majority of them did not make it in an environment focused on Patient Experience. It does not mean that they were not good managers. These people brought the concept of the "right person, wrong job" to reality. When good people find they are in the wrong job, their reasons for leaving tend to sound like "I'm tired, overwhelmed, or just not up for the effort required." While it definitely was not the hurricane that drove anyone away, it allowed us all to see who, including ourselves, was too tired, overwhelmed, or just not up for the effort required. We could see who was really on the team for the duration. As individuals began to hit their personal limits, they would leave. It felt like we were in a position that seemed like starting over every six months or so. Good people always leave something positive behind. Each one of them left something behind, whether it was a success they had led,

---

* Manually holding intravenous equipment instead of placing it on poles as would normally be the case. This meant coordinated movement and extreme care in handling the patient.

a lesson we learned, or sometimes just a chuckle. They did not leave immediately after the hurricane episode, but the behavioral precedent was set forever during that storm.

Life seemed to stand still for Community General for a few weeks. We could not get back to normal because our community was without electricity for more than two weeks. Stores could not open, and day cares and schools could not get back in session without lights. This was a tough time for employees with children. This chain of events provided me with the most satisfying opportunity to give to the employees of my hospital I had ever experienced. I ran a day care for the children of the employees that were working. For seventeen days, I fed, rocked, and played with those kids. I even got to be the tooth fairy for one of them! On the seventeenth day, we closed the day care, and I was feeling exhausted. As I got to my car, an employee stopped me and said, "Whatever happens, we know you care." That was what it was all about. All of the magic needed for this transformation was loaded in those six words. I could see these people would go to the ends of the earth if we just show them we care.

During that time, our administrators showed they cared as well. There was a shortage of fuel, ice, and water in the area. Our CEO approved to have trucks of ice and water delivered to the hospital for employees to take home and a fuel truck available to make sure employees could get gas. … He did not stop there, though. He and his administrative team loaded the ice and water into the employees' vehicles and then pulled them forward and pumped gas into their cars. The hurricane was really a turning point in servant leadership for us. The example had been set. If you could not lead with that respect and care, this would not be the place for you.

The position of patient access director became available soon after the hurricane. I was asked to assume the role in addition to my current role. I gladly accepted. Not only would it lead to more opportunities to put into place the things I had been taught by Qaalfa and my previous work, but also success would put credibility behind my ideas. I would no longer be the idea lady; I would be the implementer. I wanted to do this for my community and patients, but I wanted to be part of this CEO's success. I wanted to give back to him as he had given to me. I just hoped that I could lead a team in a manner that would cause them to want to succeed with me.

Greg: The CEO backed me.

I had heard about the theory of servant leadership but had never really given it much thought. I was seeing it on a daily basis with our admin team. They were wherever they were needed. They made us step up to the plate but supported us while doing it. My CEO could see that I had taken his directive seriously. I was getting results, but they were still coming in a little slow. The system leader for imaging services came to our CEO one day and shared that he wanted to replace me with one of his proven leaders from the system. The department was going through a lot of change, like daily team "huddles," or a gathering of the team to be updated on events, share ideas, and recognize one another. Even though it was change for the better, the doctors were not convinced these were the right changes to make. The doctors were good guys, and they had the best of intentions of doing right by our hospital. They just did not agree with the changes I had been implementing. In response, they felt getting rid of me would be easier than making the changes I thought needed to be made. They took their concerns to the system leadership. Since I did not have a well-established, long-term relationship with the system imaging services leader like others in the system,* he saw this as an opportunity to replace me with someone he knew. I knew that my days were numbered. I mean, if I was in the same situation, I would not gamble on me because I showed no signs to him of intending to change my ways. I had thought about leaving when this first started, but now I had changed. I was intrinsically motivated to make this Patient Experience thing a success, and I really wanted to stay. Rhonda and I had started something, and I wanted to see it through. A little while later, I learned that my CEO told the system leader that he was not interested in the offer. He said that I was the right person in the right job, and he was completely supportive of me. I was ashamed that I was not sure if I would have been that supportive of one of my team members. Now, I also wanted to succeed to thank him for his support. I was going to be the kind of leader that would inspire my team to want to be successful for me because of my support of them.

The Lesson: What You Need to Know …

Qaalfa: Cut the fanfare.
Kalina: Lead by example and JFDI.

It is said that change can come two ways: bottom up (starting from employees) or top down (top management imposes the change from on high). For change to really happen, it is necessary that both sides make adjustments. Change, the movement from a current known state to a future assumed state, incurs risk by definition.

A danger and common issue with top-down derived change is that it is often the case that employees who actually have to implement the change are resistant to it. They have not bought into the change concept because they do not understand

---

* Recall that Greg had been with Community General before the takeover by the system. Thus, his network within the system was not as well established as those who had been with the system in their other hospitals before the takeover.

the need, the method, or the benefit of the change. When management imposes change and employees are not onboard, the organization becomes slow, resources are used ineffectively and inefficiently, and delivery quality declines. In the worst cases, the organization decides the continued cost of attempting to achieve the change is not worth the effort. The organization ceases the change effort and writes off the cost accrued.

Bottom-up derived change generally fares much better, but of course, this change rarely happens without the support of senior management or a powerful ally within the senior ranks. When the troops are hungry for change and look for it, they can easily become discouraged when the organization (i.e., top management) is not responsive enough.

Without senior management support, there will be little to no budget to support the bottom-up change. Obviously, it is next to impossible to enact sweeping organization-wide changes without access to organization-wide resources. There are instances when this can be overcome with a groundswell of bottom-up support (e.g., union action), but this is relatively rare. Most commonly, bottom-up change without senior support leads to increased employee dissatisfaction as employees become hyperaware of a point or points that need addressing and for which they have a solution—but management ignores these. This tends to lead to high rates of turnover. If the dissatisfaction goes unchecked for a period of time, a general malaise will set in, resulting in minimal levels of productivity and service quality.

To minimize the risk inherent in all change programs, whether top down or bottom up, leadership is crucial. Leaders need to set direction, keep the focus, generate excitement, educate, and channel the energy of the troops in a productive way. Leadership is where the vision of the future direction on what is good or not and the source of hope and inspiration for action derive.

Do not be confused; leadership is much more than having the strategic idea. True leadership is modeled. As Richard Pascale, put it: "Managers do things right, leaders do the right things."*

There are many definitions that for the most part agree on what the concept of leadership means. One common definition is that leadership is organizing a group of people to achieve a common goal. But, there is more to leadership than just organizing people toward a common goal. It also includes the following:

1. The ability to create capacity, which implies developing and growing potential, whether it be people or resources; and
2. Doing something different and better, which implies that leaders are generators of change toward a future that would not happen naturally or not at a normal pace. They have a vision that others do not see, a vision that is desired once presented.

---

* As found in *The Essential Drucker: Management, the Individual and Society* (Butterworth-Heinemann, 2001).

The type of leadership that best suits a customer experience transformation is servant leadership. The phrase *servant leadership* was coined in 1970 by Robert K. Greenleaf.* He stated that:

> The servant-leader is servant first. … It begins with the natural feeling that one wants to serve, to serve first. Then conscious choice brings one to aspire to lead. That person is sharply different from one who is leader first; perhaps because of the need to assuage an unusual power drive or to acquire material possessions. …The leader-first and the servant-first are two extreme types. Between them there are shadings and blends that are part of the infinite variety of human nature.

As a leader, your colleagues and subordinates are your customers, just as patients are your employee's customers. Apply a bit of "field-of-dreams"† leadership: Build it, and they will come. This means you will need to serve as an inspiration, an example, to others no matter where they sit in the organization, whether below, across, or above you.

This is exactly the kind of leadership that the CEO of the hospital demonstrated to Rhonda, Greg, and everyone during the hurricane episode. Indeed, the pulling together showed what true service leadership was all about: The more modeling done, the more risk mitigated. Employees who model the new behaviors will inherently understand where and how to channel their efforts. The hurricane provided a crisis moment that brought things to a head, a focal point where everyone was perhaps more focused and attuned than normal. Tragedies, as unfortunate as they are, can serve as a sort of opportunity if taken. Of course, a change strategy cannot and should not be dependent on an unfortunate act of nature and the like. So, how can service leadership be demonstrated when there is no acute external focal point like a hurricane to handle?

A manager needs to do the following basic things to lead:

■ **Make a clear statement** that you are committing to the full Patient and Employee Experience—the rational and the emotional. Of course, to do this, it is necessary first to understand what being patient centric means and the resulting implications. Once this understanding is in place, it will be easy to give the troops consistent messages about what is going on and why. It is also crucial to display the behavior. Consistency is key. Inconsistency sends mixed messages and will halt a cultural transformation dead in its tracks. This first

---

* L. C. Spears, 2002, Tracing the past, present, and future of servant-leadership. In *Focus on Leadership: Servant-Leadership for the Twenty-First Century* (pp. 1–10). Wiley, New York.
† *Field of Dreams*, is a 1989 American fantasy-drama film directed by Phil Alden Robinson and is from the novel *Shoeless Joe* by W. P. Kinsella. "If you build it, he will come" is a famous line in the movie. http://en.wikipedia.org/wiki/Field_of_Dreams

step is simply to start publicly and on a regular basis talking about Patient Experience and what it means; ask questions, encourage questions, and try to answer them with employees. Make Customer Experience part of regular presentations, evaluations, and communications. Even if you are having a meeting about the legal policies, the information technology systems, or any other seemingly unrelated topic, make it related to Customer Experience. More important, when you are about to make a decision that goes against customer centricity but feel it is necessary at the moment, state it. Admit it and be clear that Patient Experience has not been forgotten. Of course, time will tell if these decisions predominate, but at least you will be conscious about your intent and seriousness about Patient Experience.

■ **Provide the experience** you want your employees to deliver. The CEO's servant leadership caught Rhonda and Greg's attention. If you want employees to be responsive, creative, and caring, demonstrate it first. Measure yourself against it and be honest with yourself about how consistent your deeds are. If you can, have someone from the outside give you a realistic assessment. One way of assessing yourself is by listening to the stories people tell about you. Which of your actions is most talked about?

■ **"JFDI"* without all of the fanfare.** You should carry out the behaviors without a megaphone yelling, "Do you guys see what I am doing here?" You can believe the troops notice what management does. Leadership is about words and action. The only time you should speak loudly about your role is when genuinely asking for employee feedback. Otherwise, speak out loud about customers, not yourself.

At Community General, the CEO demonstrated these three points.

■ He confronted one of his highest financial performers, Greg, to reassess his work in light of the Patient Experience and required him to focus on patient satisfaction also, even though at that point HCAHPS (Hospital Consumer Assessment of Healthcare Providers and Systems) reimbursement was not yet a factor. Making a clear statement in this case meant following through on the talk with adjusting rewards and recognition to account for patient satisfaction as well as financial and clinical performance.

■ He stepped in to fill the role of an absent ED tech. Rhonda happened to witness it directly, but the act made an impact even on those who did not witness it. The news (message) was carried swiftly through the informal grapevine and still lives.

■ He saw and showed his appreciation for the sacrifice employees were making to keep the hospital going as close to normal as possible during the hurricane.

---

* Just freakin' do it. Many people substitute "freaking" with a more powerful word beginning with the same letter.

He made arrangements to secure scarce resources (water and gas) for them and personally helped distribute them.

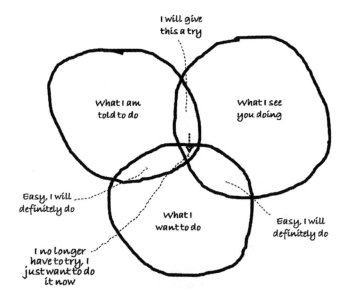

Significant change is never easy. Change implies that we are asking people to do something different from the way they normally would. The figure outlines how an employee approaches it. If change were about getting people to do exactly as they already want and know how to do, then it would be easy. Customer, including Patient, Experience means doing some things in a different way. The goal is to model (say and do) those things so employees can process what successful behavior looks like and understand why. If you offer repeated helpings of this to them, there is a great likelihood that they will internalize the ethos and behavior. When that happens, employees will help promulgate the new culture by "culture modeling it" for coworkers, and that is how the culture will be sustained.

Keep in mind the following as you begin:

■ **Be persistent**. So many programs and great ideas have failed simply because the organization was not persistent enough in pursuing the goal. This is essentially a waste of money. Presuming you have made a clear statement and are becoming increasingly comfortable in serving your employees, here are three scenarios in which you are at risk of breaking your promise:

– *Unexpected success:* Often, organizations are surprised by the quick results a positive transformation can bring. This is not uncommon when the change is centered on improving the Customer Experience. It often happens when there has been performance so poor that "getting the basics right" sounds like a huge step to the organization. In these cases, the quick wins can give a false sense of security about the speed and traction of the change. The risk is that the leadership may take this as evidence that further concerted effort and resources are not as much a priority, and the movement will carry on with less support and effort. Cultural transformation requires constant nurturing. It is about the journey much more than a particular destination. Each step pushes the bar further with added enthusiasm.

- *Unexpected crisis:* As in the accounts of Rhonda and Greg, unforeseen circumstances can easily throw people off track. Under stress, people tend to resort immediately to their most established and familiar mode of behavior. Be prepared for a crisis from the start. Crisis can mean anything from a rebellion in a meeting to a hurricane. At times like that, the common excuse is: "We'll get to it right after we are done with this." As often as possible, ask yourself how any decision affects your Customer Experience. If you are forced to cut corners because of the circumstances, do not assume it is obvious to everyone why that had to be done. Demonstrate that even when tough decisions have to be made, you are aware of and considering the damage they could do to the Customer Experience.

■ **Accept the cyclic nature of progress.** Even the most successful leaders and transformations will at times feel like they are not achieving progress. Cultural transformation is an iterative and constant process. It requires occasional molting. You will remember Rhonda saying: "It felt like we were in a position that seemed like starting over every six months or so." A leader's job is never done. A leader will always have the sense of needing to achieve more. However, it is necessary to recognize also the evidence of success even, or perhaps especially, when it comes in more subtle forms like the stories people tell about you and their work, the care people show toward each other as a team, a hug given by a patient to a nurse, requests made by staff that justify patient comfort and care over ease of job and execution, and so on. Cues such as these will prove invaluable during the molting phases. They will let you know that things are on the right track.

Keep in mind the words of Lao Tse, the famous Chinese philosopher who observed that

> To lead people, walk beside them. ... As for the best leaders, the people do not notice their existence. The next best, the people honor and praise. The next, the people fear; and the next, the people hate. ... When the best leader's work is done the people say, "We did it ourselves!"*

* MIT OpenCourseWare http://ocw.mit.edu; Leadership Training Institute, Summer 2008 http://ocw.mit.edu/high-school/courses/leadership-training-institute/lecture-notes-and-videos/ ltiquotes.pdf

Chapter 4

Connect to Engage

Rhonda: Purpose is the magic dust within.

Although our culture was starting to be defined, it was not yet reality. The people creating the experience and delivering the care had to see how important they were and that they contributed. When you talked to the staff, there seemed to be a theme of "I'm just a ... ." No one seemed to think they were important. There was a lack of pride. Employees tended to start sentences with, "I am just a ... ." which lessened their importance and their responsibility. It was clear that if we could not help them to connect their job to making a difference in the Patient Experience, we would not be successful.

One day when I was walking to the floors to round on the staff, I stopped so one of the men from Environmental Services could get past with a cart of linen he was taking to the floor. When he offered to let me go ahead of him, I insisted that I could not delay his important mission. He was very sincere when he explained that he was not important—that he was only a housekeeper, and I was the one that was important. Another lightbulb went on. These people weren't resistant or uncaring; they just felt unworthy. I had been asking the impossible. I had been asking them to wow people when they did not see the importance of the work they did. He saw himself as someone delivering sheets and blankets—period. He thought it stopped there. I asked him if he knew the role he played in our mission. Our mission was to make the community that we served healthier. I told him about when I was a young girl and I would get sick. The thing that always made me feel better was clean sheets. I remember snuggling up in the freshly made bed and how much better that made me feel. I went on to say that medicines and surgeries heal, but the little touches that show we care make people feel better all the way through and

33

through. He was one of those responsible for those little details like clean sheets and first impressions. Our customers see the care we put into maintaining a clean healing environment before any of us have a chance to greet them. I had seen him several times since I had joined this team. When I saw him after that conversation, he held his head high with a new sense of pride. I knew, though, that it would have to be reinforced on a consistent basis for him to keep that feeling. How was that going to be possible? I never realized how much I did not know until I started this job. I did not know how to do it, but I did know it had to be done, and that Greg and I could not do it alone.

It is funny how you get your answers when you aren't really looking. One day I was walking through the cafeteria when an employee stopped me. She wanted to tell me about a remarkable thing one of her coworkers had done. A patient was about to be discharged and did not have the proper clothing for the climate. He had no jacket, and she went and retrieved hers and gave it to the patient. I was overwhelmed by the selflessness of this act. On impulse, I sent an e-mail to the entire hospital, publicly thanking the employee for her efforts with the subject heading of "WOW." It was like throwing food to the starving masses. During that day, I received four more e-mails complimenting other people. The employees were so proud to have a venue to share their good deeds. I started to receive these stories, which came to be known as wows, by the dozens.

When I sent the e-mailed compliments out, they were not just accepted by all. It was so odd to me that people would worry about me sending out too many compliments. From some, the feedback was that we were thanking people for doing their job. I stood firm in my opinion that thanking someone for doing their job well was a good thing. It reminded me of my grandmother. When I became engaged, she only gave me one piece of advice. She told me never to stop saying thank you. She said to thank him when he opened the door for me, when he went to work, and when he played with the kids. She said to thank him for whatever he did that I wanted him to keep doing. So, the wow mentality was born. It was the first step to making appreciation one of the characteristics of our new culture.

It was working, so I wanted to maximize it. A friend shared that she thought *wow* stood for working on wonderful. Soon afterward, that was adapted further, and "I Work on Wonderful Every Day," or "iWoWed" became a full program. Any compliment that I received, whether by phone, letter, or in person and whether from a customer, physician, or employee was known as a wow. We began tracking wows by employee.

About this time, we started another initiative that we called Caregiver Cards. The idea was a card that would be started at the patient's first point of contact and would follow them throughout their stay. The purpose was so the patient could have the names of all those who cared for them. Not only would it make us more accountable, but also it would give the patient an opportunity to thank us by name. One day, we received a letter from a patient that mentioned more than twenty employees by name. The CEO [chief executive officer] and I were reading it when we decided to do something big with the letter. I always wanted to do something big! He was more reserved by nature than I was, but he always got caught up in the excitement. Soon, the operator paged those twenty-something names one by one over the loudspeaker with a request to report to the cafeteria. The directors and managers were also asked to come. Very quickly, the cafeteria was filling up with a completely baffled group of employees. The directors were lined up against the wall like a receiving line. As the employees entered, we all applauded them. Everyone was looking to each other for an explanation. The CEO stepped up on a chair and began reading the letter. After he was finished, he went to each of those employees, took their hand, and thanked them for making a difference in this patient's life. After several of these opportunities to thank the team, the employees were beginning to engage in this effort with us. When the chiefs would round, they took advantage of every chance to thank someone for making a difference.

They were also pretty open when something was out of sorts. One day, when the CEO was rounding on a nursing unit, he found a patient curled up in a fetal position, undressed, and with no cover. When he asked the nurse why the patient appeared so uncared for, the nurse flippantly explained that the patient was an addict and was going through withdrawal, and that his behavior got him where he was. The CEO immediately took this real-time opportunity to teach this employee that one of our behaviors was respect, and that he would respect the patient no matter how they became ill. The message was becoming clear to us all. Either you were engaged with our values or mission or you were not taking care of our patients. There was another time when the CEO was rounding in the Emergency Department. A nurse with more than twenty years of employment at our hospital gave it to him straight. She let him know that she had no intentions of changing. The patients were lucky she was here to care for them, and she would not bow down to them. He asked her to gather her things and leave and told her not to return. It sent a message to everyone. He was thankful and supportive, but they were accountable. The expectations were set that it was not enough to be good at your technical or clinical skills alone. You had to be the entire package of those skills combined with your care for people and your ability to show it. The midlevel leaders saw his example and started acting accordingly. Soon, many of the leaders were holding people to all of the standards.

Greg: Move it from me to we.

One day when I opened my e-mail, I saw a message from Rhonda with the subject of WOW. It was an e-mail sent to the entire hospital telling the story of how an employee made a difference for a patient. I thought, "Wow is right"; this was different. Historically, e-mail and staff meetings were used to report the bad things that were happening. Soon after that, we reported to the cafeteria to listen to the CEO read a letter complimenting several of the employees. The people mentioned in that letter were really excited about hearing the message. The wheels in my mind started turning. If my department and I personally were to be successful, I would need energy from the people doing the work. Engagement was a new word to me and in my environment, but it was really starting to make sense. I had proven I could get people to do individual tasks well, but this was bigger than that. It was going to take full commitment of the team to get these results.

I had hired a new manager, and she was great. She was communicating with the team and adding fun to the daily grind. As my own leadership style reverted back to what I learned in high school sports, I remembered that if you wanted someone to improve their skills, you needed to make them feel involved, like they were contributing. Traditionally, we had a director and manager making decisions and owning processes. Frontline staff took orders and completed studies, but that was their only part in operations. We had team leads in each modality. They were there to manage daily activities, but their input was never important. They were there to perform their duties without any desire to improve or change. They had no ownership of the successes or failures in their areas. This was the first order of change. The manager and I called the team leads together in a formal team leader meeting. We really shared information with them. Not only did they know the performance on the goals, but also they knew what contributed to those outcomes. Prior to this, we had shared the number results for all of our goals but not the actions that led to those numbers. We only gave basic information but no detail. That had all changed. Now, we were giving them the outcomes and letting them tell us the actions that would make them change for the positive. At first, they were reluctant to share. It was like any other trust situation—we would have to earn it.

I realized in that meeting there was a big gap that would need to be closed. The team leads had to feel important. They had to know this place could make it or break it on their watch. They not only had to feel responsibility but also had to feel their importance. What I had learned is the impact their contribution could make. We had already begun the work on motivation, so now we had to hand them over the keys and let this place truly be theirs. There were little secrets in our department. Previously, as management I felt reluctant to share information about the organization and our department. I even withheld information about things that directly impacted the staff, like layoffs and pay cuts. Now, I knew that had I involved them and asked for their solutions, layoffs and pay cuts may not have been needed. In this new culture, closed-door meetings were reserved to protect their privacy, not to keep things from them. We showed them the gap, and they did the research on the causes. Just as we were involving them, the team leads were to involve everyone in their area in all communication. The hospital had rolled out a program called the Daily Huddle in which each department was to meet together for five minutes on each shift and communicate about things going on in the hospital. This was not a shift report; instead, it was transparency of information. Those huddles were to occur department-wide each morning and evening. Most people enjoyed the sharing of information, but of course there were those that hid out, too. We had the team leaders engaged, though. Some staff members may have been able to hide from me, but they would have trouble hiding from their team lead. Soon, the entire team was participating. The communication spread outside the huddle as well. Throughout the day, you could see team leads asking advice and sharing information with the members of their team. A team, that is what we were becoming.

It was also very evident which departments were not participating in the huddle. Administration became aware of this and began dropping in at huddle time. Soon, huddles were a part of the daily activities across the entire building.

Communication was happening, but sometimes it was chaotic and led to different messages. We needed some structure. In the past, I would have probably created a plan and started with a formal program and not started with the water cooler conversations. I would have had a meeting and rolled out this communication plan and the expectations around compliance. In hindsight, it was better to get the information flowing and the sharing of ideas happening in a comfortable environment and then bring in the formal communication tools. Otherwise, the formality may have been stifling. Now, we were successful in the effort of communicating, and everyone trusted me enough to speak up. It was time to put some structure in place to make sure that we sustained our improvements.

The first formal change was with the staff meetings. First of all, they became team meetings where information was not only shared with team members but also by them. Our CEO met with the leadership team monthly and shared what was going on in the hospital. I began to share that at our meetings as well, and then as a team we discussed our contribution to the good of the whole. For example, if we were talking about the hospital performance for patient safety, we gathered the teams' ideas for how they could improve the outcomes or celebrate our success. The meetings became a real war room mentality where we celebrated our successes and developed resolutions for our challenges. In one of the earliest team meetings, we were talking about supply costs. These costs had been out of control for a long time. Each modality ordered their own supplies, and there were a lot of inconsistencies with stockpiles of inventory in each area. One employee stepped up to the plate. She shared some great ideas and took ownership of ordering supplies for the whole department. She became an expert at the subject. She worked with the individual modalities to set par levels and standardize what was ordered. Supply costs began trending down, and soon we were celebrating 100 percent improvement in an area where we had previously failed. These results could be tied to the engagement of one employee taking the lead and working with everyone else. This was an employee with no leadership title who had led us to success.

Team meetings were great for monthly communication, but we needed information to be shared daily. We already had the Daily Huddles, but we needed a place where the information was in writing and for all to see. We had a lot of conversations going on with the team leads and the team members. I wanted to make sure there was a consistent message from me present. What I needed was a board where I could post things that I wanted everyone to see. In Imaging Services, everything happens in the quality control room. It serves as the hub for the department, and everything revolves around it. In the middle of that hub, we put up a board that was about four feet tall and eight feet long. Now, I had to figure out what I wanted to put on it. I put information about the departmental goals and results by modality. As I watched my team read the information, I saw that they were really supportive in getting the results, but something was missing. I realized that even though I was including them in so much, they had never been asked about the departmental goals. How could I expect them to deliver on some really tall expectations if they weren't a part of setting them?

At the next team meeting, we talked about goals. It was not an information push; it was a gathering of ideas. I concentrated on tying their daily tasks to the bigger picture. The system we joined had a well-formed identity that defined a mission that was achieved through employee behaviors that led to success around six strategies. During this meeting, our place within that identity was found. We linked the work that we did with the greater goal of the system. We did this for each of the six strategies until each employee could relate their efforts to the identity of the system. I shared best practices in the system and the nation compared to where we were. The team created their own goals. I was surprised to find they actually set them higher than I would have. The difference was tangible in the way that group worked together to achieve their goals. More important than the goals that were set was the way we left all sharing a name. Whenever the name of the system we worked for was spoken, it was as if it was our own name being said. We were no longer individuals, but we were now part of a greater good.

The challenge now shifted from within our department to the departments we worked with. While we identified with the greater name, that connection was still not made across our hospital. There was still no consistency among the departments, and that was painfully obvious to my team. When they were working with other departments, they began to take it as a betrayal when they did not see the same ownership they felt. They felt empowered in their own environment to correct one another when they slacked off; that comfort was not felt when the slacker worked in another area. I was reminded again that I could not stop with my own direct reports. What had been a directive by my CEO to get my own department in order became a much bigger personal goal. I needed to talk this over with Rhonda so we could get movement across the hospital.

Rhonda: Calibrate the teams.

Greg was making tremendous strides in his area. One of the problems when one area shapes up is it becomes blindingly evident that other areas are not. The departments with engaged employees stood out. The way he was gaining that success was through connection and communication. His employees were connecting to the identity of the hospital and proud to be a part of the successes. One of the danger points could be building silos. If each department became successful within itself, oblivious to what was going on in the other areas; you would end up with a dysfunctional group of departments that resented each other rather than working together. To push for consistency, a template with mandatory team meeting information was created. The method of delivery was optional—there was a PowerPoint, an outline, and so on. The bottom line was, like the Daily Huddle, the information had to get out, and the message had to be consistent department to department.

A group of engaged directors was called together by the CEO; they worked to develop the practices that were intended to make us the best place to work, practice medicine, and receive care. When stated in that way, it seemed simple, but it was really a big effort before us. One of the initiatives developed by this team was the meeting template. The team created an agenda that covered the six strategies and hospital news. For each strategy, there was a slide that covered the hospital performance and activities for that strategy. Following that slide was a department-specific slide that was completed within that department. There were also slides dedicated to recognition and news you can use. As the tools were being implemented, you could almost feel the tide turning. Just like with the huddle, it was becoming very clear who was using this tool and who was not. It was beginning to be difficult to hide in the masses of the disengaged because they were becoming fewer.

Sometimes, though, it felt like it was one step forward and two steps backward when it came to creating the right team. We had started using some best practice techniques for talent acquisition, such as peer interviewing and selection for service interview questions. We were beginning to get some good talent in the door. We soon learned, though, that everyone already onboard was not living the change. Often, when one of these great new hires got in the trenches with some of the less-engaged people, they were at risk. Not only was the risk that they would leave, but also there was a chance they could be influenced to become a part of "that" team, the team of resistance. We needed to get a clear message to them at the point of entry. We began an onboarding packet that each leader was expected to use starting at the interview and going through the first year of employment. The leadership group also developed a workshop on service to be attended at about the thirtieth day of employment to reiterate the message of our expectations.

The Lesson: What You Need to Know ...

Qaalfa: Channel already occurring target behaviors.
Kalina: Learn to tie an Engagement Bowtie.

Previously, we spoke about motivating employees by appealing to their "caregiver" persona and getting them to see the Patient Experience as patients do so that they can relate to it. Here, we talk about the jump from getting employees excited to getting them to invest effort in the "right" direction—a direction that is aligned with the Customer Experience strategy.

Motivation is the first step to getting people interested in the matter you are trying you push. But, motivation alone will not do the trick. Zig Ziglar,[*] whom Rhonda often quotes, once said: "People often say that motivation doesn't last. Well, neither does bathing—that's why we recommend it daily." A motivated employee is a great start (the only start really), but an engaged employee is a move forward. Motivation is reason behind a decision. Engagement is taking action on the decision in a way that benefits the organization. With engagement you give a motivated employee momentum.

One definition of engagement in the workplace is that it is "a positive attitude held by the employee toward the organization and its values. An engaged employee is aware of business context and works with colleagues to improve performance within the job for the benefit of the organization."[†] There is a body of research that shows that engaged employees are associated with greater productivity and profit. A 2009 U.K.-based study[‡] conducted with National Health Service employees showed that highly engaged staffs are

- More likely to be reported as providing a high-quality service
- More likely to have higher ratings on higher overall performance
- Less likely to have higher rates of sickness and absenteeism

The difference between motivating an employee and engaging one is measured in the direction and persistence of their effort. A motivated employee feels the urge to do something; an engaged employee feels the urge to do something for the benefit of the organization.

Motivation can be achieved by appealing to an individual's personal value system; engagement is achieved by relating that system to the work environment and organization. It becomes clear that simply appealing to the employee's values will not often produce company-aligned results. Employees who are motivated will have good intentions to do the right thing, but in many instances without engagement, they can only do the best thing according to their personal interpretation of best. In a professional environment, this personal interpretation of best will almost always be positive; it just may not necessarily be aligned with the organization's strategy. A common outcome of having employees who are more motivated

---

[*] http://thinkexist.com/quotes/zig_ziglar/

[†] Robinson, D., Perryman, S., and Hayday, S., Report 408, Institute of Employee Studies, April 2004.

[‡] NHS Employers, 2010, November 22. New analysis shows staff engagement brings wider benefits. http://www.nhsemployers.org/EmploymentPolicyAndPractice/staff-engagement/researchandreports/Pages/HighengagementscoreslinktofinancialefficienciesintheNHS.aspx (accessed November 2012).

than engaged is that they can work on slightly different planes. The end result is a Customer Experience that is not consistent even if it is positive.

Likewise, getting employees simply to understand the business strategy alone will not lead to behavioral change that lasts beyond the times employees believe they are being monitored. You obtain something of a Hawthorne effect when there is engagement without appropriate motivation. You may recall that the Hawthorne effect refers to the increased productivity of workers while they are being observed. In the original experiment at the Hawthorne Works plant of Western Electric that was carried out in the late 1920s and early 1930s, researchers were interested in how various lighting conditions affected worker efficiency. What they found serendipitously, however, was that positive effects witnessed seemed to be more dependent on workers being observed rather than the lighting variations.

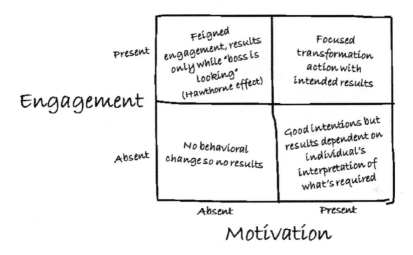

Keep in mind that we tend to be vigilant in paying attention, monitoring, or measuring the early stages of a transformation program. The implication is that as a result of this vigilance, you may need to take the Hawthorne effect into account. Your vigilance may result in positive effects. Do not assume that early positive results in areas you are monitoring equate to engagement success. You will need to do some stealth monitoring to get a true sense of the level of engagement.

Motivation and engagement both are very personal and also bring the sense of reward to the individual; the first may relate to different things (money, safety, respect, freedom, etc.), and the second one relates specifically to the organization. Rhonda mentioned the story of telling one of the housekeepers how important he was to the hospital in very personal terms. She succeeded not only by delivering a standard message but also in personalizing it and his place in that story. She allowed him to see the connection between his own values and his role at the hospital. His sense of pride blossomed after that and so did his performance. She went on to say that she knew that this connection message would have to be continually reinforced. In other words, the trick was not delivering the connection message in a training module or skills lab. It happened on the floor where the work was being performed. It is significant that Rhonda chose to highlight a person from Environmental Services—a housekeeper—because it shows that this work is for all employees, not just those who you might first think would be worth the effort (e.g., givers of direct care in a hospital). Rhonda was constantly giving these messages to individuals she ran across throughout the hospital. This is exactly what is needed to turn motivation into engagement.

A first step is to help employees see their role and themselves as relevant to the Customer Experience. To be honest, it will be difficult to make that personal connection for all the clusters of roles you will run across in your organization. It is often not straightforward to articulate how certain roles actually do fit and contribute to the Customer Experience in a way that connects. But, if you cannot do it, do not expect the disengaged employee to do it either. One of your primary roles is to make that connection real for employees. This will take effort on your part. This is one of those things that take a lot of effort that at first may not seem worth it. In other words, it is one of those most commonly skipped parts of a cultural transformation. Here is what you should do:

- Develop a list of key experiences customers have at your organization. Write these up as full-blown, character-rich stories or at least have them at the ready in your mental database.
- Create a list of role clusters at your organization. If you work at a large company, it will not be every role. Rather, it may be something like departments.
- For each of these role clusters, think of how its function has an impact on one or more of your stories. Be sure to personify the story. Make it personal if you can but tell it on the human level. Do not tell it in charts, graphs, and figures. Or have a pool of Customer Experience stories.
- Then, repeat, repeat, repeat—until it is déjà vu all over again as Yogi Berra* famously once said.

However, most of what Rhonda and Greg wrote about was how to make employees move from being individually connected to being a team of connected employees. Most people want to jump to the activities that do this. They often neglect the motivation efforts mentioned previously. If this mistake is made, the result will likely lead to some form of the Hawthorne effect as your team engagement efforts will likely be successful as long as you are vigilantly monitoring the situation.

Rhonda often says: "I also knew that even if I were as consistent as I could be, I would not always be there to deliver these messages to each and every employee in the organization. I needed employees to keep it going, to pick up the slack even

---

* Yogi Berra was a great American baseball player famous for his clever quips. "It ain't over 'til it's over" is often quoted and is arguably the most famous example. Simultaneously denying and confirming his reputation, Berra once stated, "I really didn't say everything I said."

when I was not around." Greg has told us: "If my department and I personally were to be successful, I would need energy from the people doing the work." This part of engagement is more public, and its purpose is to get employees to feel comfortable and indeed share responsibility for what others are doing. So, how do you make this a team practice versus an individual practice? The answer lies in the way you engage employees.

There are two central elements or drivers of engagement: appreciation and active listening. Appreciation is the extent to which the organization is concerned for employees as human beings. Active listening is the extent to which management pays attention to the efforts and behaviors that lead to the intended customer experience.

Appreciation

It is absolutely crucial that employees feel valued by the organization and see themselves as such. The key phrase here is *feel valued*. Employees are most often told they are valued, but this usually carries little weight with them. They need to *feel* valued for it to be meaningful, which means you will have to convince them they that are valued. Telling them once is not enough. Continuous action is required. It is also how you tell them that will be the difference between them picking up the feeling or not. While you may only be talking, your actions of doing this informally at every opportunity with all levels and classes of employees is what will make the impression. That impression serves as the groundwork for engaging the team.

Once the individual employees take onboard the message that all sorts of roles and role-specific behaviors are being informally and sincerely appreciated by you, they will begin to see such behaviors in those around them. At some point, if given the chance, they will want those close to them to be recognized for the great job they have been doing. This is exactly what happened when Rhonda opened the floodgates by writing that e-mail to tell everyone about the employee who did the extraordinary thing by giving her coat to a discharged patient who did not have one with him. Other employees started sending Rhonda examples of their own to share in a similar fashion. Rhonda, of course, reacted to this opening of the floodgates, and the iWoWed concept was born.

What may not come across easily is that appreciation should not only apply to actions that go "the extra mile" and are "out of the ordinary." It applies to everyday tasks done with the right intent in mind. It is not so much that the nurse gave the coat to the patient, but that she found a way to show care—the experience the hospital wants to deliver—even without the guidelines and training behind it. Appreciation refers to acknowledging that employees are doing their job with the proper intent behind it and are finding ways to convey that intent.

To a large extent, employees assess the sincerity of the acts of appreciation based on what, when, and who is being appreciated. They will be left with a gut feeling of sincere appreciation from the cues given by you during the continuous action. What you are saying hits them on the rational level, but the who, when, and where you are saying it to (i.e., the continuous action for all kinds of employees) is what hits them on the gut emotional level.

Employees are sensitive to who gets the appreciation. It is a death knell of your transformation efforts if employees come to feel/understand that the appreciation is reserved for select clusters of employees like the frontline employees or those who already have some sort of visibility. You will have already overcome this hurdle if you have been continuously delivering your "connection" message and while doing so are giving a sincere thanks to employees who demonstrate the behaviors aligned with your customer experience efforts.

Employees will also be sensitive to the battle that likely will be going on within the management ranks in the early days of your transformation. Employees (and you) will know that some managers will have the mentality that the employee-worker relationship is an economic transaction. That is, it is an equal exchange: The business pays the salary, and the employee does work. In other words, those managers will see their responsibility as a financial one to the employee. Any other demands are distant and secondary at best. Such managers will not see the benefit of showing appreciation to employees for doing the jobs they were hired to do. This attitude works well in the world of perfect economies or when applied to machines. It does not work well when people are involved because people have feelings. This mentality, when acted on by managers, may get employees to do tasks—especially while management is looking—but employees will be unlikely to go the extra mile. Cultural transformation requires determined effort. This effort is what we mean by going the extra mile.

Active Observation/Listening

Active observation/listening is perhaps an obvious requirement. It is how you become aware of the occurrence of those behaviors aligned with Customer Experience. You will only be able to appreciate behaviors that somehow come to your attention. You will do this either by direct observation or by hearing about it from others.

These behaviors may be occurring now in your organization. However, if no one is paying attention and then following up with appreciation, the behavior is likely to be sporadic at best. If, on the other hand, that behavior is noticed and subsequently appreciated, the behavior will be encouraged. To put it another way, you cannot appreciate correct behavior if you have not identified any correct behaviors. The root cause of not having identified what the correct behavior is can be either that the behaviors have not been occurring at all or that you have not been actively looking. In general, the second is the culprit. Rhonda and Greg used Daily Huddles, monthly team meetings, and pushpin boards to capture these behaviors. Companies we have worked with use methods involving their intranet, phone apps, Skype, and so on. The method of capture is secondary. The point is to actively notice the aligned behaviors or attempted behaviors as this will provide you with the opportunities to show appreciation to the team.

Note that there are two types of behaviors you will want to be on the lookout for as candidates for appreciation: outcome behaviors and process behaviors. Outcome behaviors are those that result in a decision that directly improves the Customer Experience. Process behaviors are those that reflect what an employee does.

Here, we emphasize listening over talking in two-way communication because most often managers have less trouble finding ways of talking at employees. It is rare for them to actively listen to employees. This is what Greg described when he stated that even though his team meetings and pushpin board were great avenues for him to get his message across to his employees, he found something lacking in them. It was not until he opened up these communication channels as listening avenues with the employees doing the talking that his employees took ownership.

Engagement happens in two parts: personal and public. In the personal part, you will get an employee to connect the company's Customer Experience strategy to the employee's personal motivation. Employees become more motivated when this connection has been made. When this connection is made, employees will feel their job is rewarding in intangible ways. This is an intimate feeling, however. You will need to do the public part to increase the likelihood that the target behaviors become amplified in the organization. The public part involves reacting to employees' behavior in a manner that supports their Customer Experience capacity and skills. This whole process repeated over time will increase engagement. We refer to this repeated loop of activity as the Engagement Bowtie.

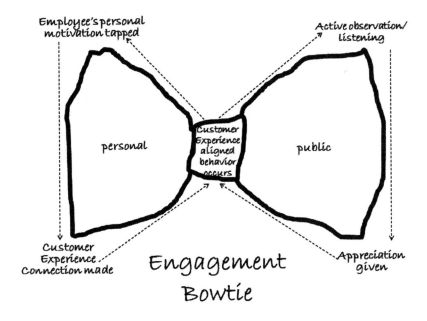

Central to the Engagement Bowtie is the fact that correct behaviors are going on in any given organization right now. What is needed on the personal side is a link between an employee's personal motivation and work behavior with the organization's Customer Experience strategy.

What is required on the public side is that those target behaviors are highlighted and then appreciated. The effect of repeating this action is that employees will begin to model the public loop with their immediate coworkers. This builds working teams aligned with Customer Experience.

With continued repeated loop iterations, these experience-aligned teams will begin to identify and appreciate target behaviors in other teams. So, over time the engagement starts out small, with an individual spark here and there. That grows and feeds on itself until it reaches a tipping point within a group of colleagues, and they form a Customer Experience-oriented team. Ultimately, these teams will begin to look across the organization to appreciate target behaviors wherever they occur. This is in fact one of the ultimate goals in a cultural transformation.

Engagement does not happen overnight. Employees will have "good" days (days when they feel engaged and eager) and "bad" days (days when they just cannot wait until they get home). Then, the good days will start to ever so slightly outnumber the bad days until finally good days are just "usual days."

Chapter 5

Fail, Then Account

Greg: Watch out for Phase 4!

The progress was happening in about four different parts or phases—awareness, learning, application of the knowledge, and maintenance.

Phase 1 was simply awareness. Once I started communicating, the goals were developed and enough of our team got onboard to start seeing movement. This did not take us to where we needed to be, but it greased the wheels and started them turning. Once we had a significant amount of our team aligned, they became eager students soaking in as much knowledge as they could. Phase 2 was the learning phase. The team members owned the improvement challenge, so they were eager to make it work. This phase was all about learning to put structure behind the efforts. Unfortunately, in this phase we saw our results become inconsistent. As we tried new things and people's energy leveled off, our scores would dip and rise. It would have been my normal tendency to stop here. It is kind of like when you go on a diet and lose the weight you need to lose but then stop doing the changes, and you gain the lost weight back plus more. You end up worse off than before you made the changes. On top of it all, it affects your morale. I had made that mistake before and was determined to make these changes stick. I had to keep with it until it became the culture Rhonda was always referring to. If my favorite word is *accountability*; hers is *culture*.

In Phase 3, we became content experts and began to apply that content. By now, we had learned what worked and what did not work in our environment. We tried different initiatives and ways of doing those initiatives. We quickly went through Phases 1 and 2, and the team owned the success. They were champions. One thing we had learned was that if you want to know what the customer wants, you need to ask the customer. Our team looked at every patient satisfaction survey and attributed it to the team members who had cared for that patient. The team could tell how each employee had contributed to the whole. They called many patients and asked for specific feedback. If one of my team members had failed that patient, they apologized. If a department we worked with let the patient down, they called them on it. They held themselves and their partnering departments responsible for the outcomes. They took no prisoners and no excuses. This was not me calling; this was the frontline team. Their involvement was the turning point. They were engaged, and they knew what to do. Now they were applying that knowledge. It was not until we reached this phase that we actually reached our goal.

Phase 4 hit us like a ton of bricks. We had learned what we needed to know, we had implemented, but now we needed to maintain. It was a bit shocking the first time we experienced failure after many months of success. It happened to us when we let our guard down. We started taking the new culture for granted. When one of our key players left, the person was replaced by an employee from another department who was not as engaged. We took it for granted that this person would catch on without effort from us and let the new member drag us backward—just a little. It did not take long for us to bounce back. The team did not like the feeling of failing after so much success. The team quickly stepped into action and coached that person into submission. We had experienced success and were not about to go back.

Rhonda: Each day is a new start.

Greg and I had become comrades in all of this, but there was also a little bit of healthy competition. I had just been given the role of leadership over a team that had not participated in the transition into the new culture. They had been protected from the change by their previous leader. I saw that it had taken Greg a little over a year to reach his success. I also took note that all of the departments throughout the building were not at the same place in transition. The reality was, though, that no team was as advanced as Greg's, and I refused to be shown up by him. This transition was a little challenging for me as well. In my expanded role, I would no longer report directly to the CEO [chief executive officer] who I had become to trust so much. I had to get over it, though, because I had accepted this position. In the words of my ten-year-old daughter, I had to "Suck it up, buttercup." The reality was this group had not asked for me to be their boss either, and they were full of fear and anxiety mixed with a little anger and resentment. I intended for them to welcome me with open minds and open arms.

Surprisingly, the resistance was not as strong as I anticipated, and they were eager to do well. I just had to build trust with them by being honest. On day one,

I addressed their fears and told them I wanted nothing more than for them to be a success. They were surprised that I realized how they felt. A large part of the wall was broken down in that first conversation. Like the housekeeper I had encountered in the hallway, this group was unaware of their importance to the whole picture. Each day, I shared examples of how their contribution affected the entire hospital. On payday, I thanked them all for collecting the money that made my paycheck possible. As the hospital business office, they were responsible for securing the patient's identity and the patient's account. They had never seen their role as significant before. The pride and worthiness they felt made the changes easier to take. I was asking them to do things that seemed impossible to them, but they made it happen. We soon took on Walt Disney's motto: "It is fun to do the impossible."

With the outward goal of adding to the hospital's success, I told my new boss I would reach success in this department in nine months. My real driver was to not be outdone by Greg. It did not take long for me to realize that my new team did not feel part of the hospital because they did not participate in the things the hospital did. They did not take part in the activities that had become part of the norm around here, like Daily Huddles, team meetings, and the iWOWed [I Work on Wonderful Every Day] program. It was not that those things did not apply to them; their leadership just had not implemented them for their area. The group had stayed just below the radar. I knew that to turn this around in such a short time span would require them to be completely immersed in the culture that had already been accepted by many of the other departments. On day one, we started with the Daily Huddle. It was also on my first day that there was a hospital recognition event. I was appalled that not one of the people from my department participated. To make it worse, they came and got the food that was offered and returned to their department to eat rather than participate in the event. I could not believe it. I was the director of Customer Experience as well as Business Services. I was in charge of the event, and it was my team that did not bother to participate in recognizing their peers but still felt entitled to the food. That started a new culture characteristic for our department. When I returned to the area, I called an emergency huddle. I had them all gather around, and I let them share in my disappointment. I am a straight shooter, and I shot a lot of holes in that room. When I finished, it became clear to everyone that participation was mandatory. I was not inappropriate—I just let them know what was expected, and that I was helping them make it happen. No excuses would be accepted, and reasons for the failure would be resolved. On that day, I think we started and finished Phase 1. Everyone was aware of the expectations, consequences, and rewards.

Whenever we had a quality or satisfaction result below our goal, the department took action. They traced every breach back to the person responsible and coached or escalated the situation. The team developed an internal training program where they identified the learning needs and created the content for the education. It was then taught by one of them. In a little more than eight months, we had reached all of our goals. Because of our success with business and customer experience outcomes, we were being asked to share our practices across our system. We had moved from being the lowest-performing hospital in our system to being at the top of the measurement spectrum. We were ninety-nine percent compliant with all of our processes and in the top one percent for all of our outcomes. Those were the numbers on the board, but the real win was in the faces of the team. They were so proud and confident. For some of them, I think this may have been the first time they experienced such a feeling of accomplishment. One hundred percent of our staff were recognized as top performers in patient satisfaction; one of our employees was named Employee of the Year, and our department won two facility awards for breakthroughs.

Our departments seemed under control with the exception of a few pockets, but after three years in the hospital, there were still daily challenges to the new culture. They may not have been as common and were certainly not accepted, but even after so much change and success, they existed. Greg and I were talking with one of our peers and friends one day. Greg and I made our teams total rule follow-ers, but this person did not. This led to resentment and made it difficult for the three teams to work together. We shared our frustration in an attempt to use peer accountability. We did not think we were heard, but that was not relevant for long. The next day, one of his employees broke a rule, resulting in patient harm. Later, when we were alone, this leader wondered aloud how this happened. It is painful to watch someone learn something the hard way, but if there is anything this experi-ence has taught me, it is that lessons learned at the school of hard knocks are not soon forgotten.

Hard knocks is exactly what I thought we might be in for when Greg shared that one of the areas in his department was not going to meet their goals for the past year. Even with all of the success as a whole, there were still challenges. This was big because as a result of this performance, they were not going to get their yearly merit increase. I started to get cold feet on the accountability thing. I mean if we held back their money, they might all leave. What would the reaction to that be? We could potentially shoot ourselves in the foot if we ran off employees whose positions would be hard to fill. Greg insisted that he was going to stick to his guns. I was worried. A lack of success in employee satisfaction was one of the things that got this movement going in the first place.

Greg: Lean on me.

I watched Rhonda's department go down the path toward success that my team had gone down before them. As she worked with her group to achieve the goals, my team focused on maintaining our success. Rhonda's team did many of the same things ours had done but at a faster pace. One difference was that Rhonda did not have to figure out what to do or where to start. Through our collaborative efforts, she went through the trial periods when my team did. It taught us the real advantage of sharing best practices. We had each other and were not in this alone. We made it a point to be there for other leaders when they struggled. Many of our leaders were still fairly new.

For both of our areas, the success could be summed up to accountability, recognition, and consistency. The practice of tying all incremental results to the tech or registration person held each of them individually responsible for their contribution to the team's outcome. Through that practice, we were able to coach when necessary and recognize when warranted. The real stickiness, though, was consistency. You could never allow for an excuse or for your staff to be victimized by their circumstances. A busy day in the emergency department does not excuse poor quality or service.

I told Rhonda that a group of my employees was not going to get a raise this year because they did not meet their performance goals. She made fun of me and felt I was getting the hammer out again. I knew it was the right thing to do. I was a little nervous because my own increase and job security included employee satisfaction and retention. Even Human Resources questioned my decision. I was too far into this now, though. I had to do what I knew was right. In the end, no one in that area got a raise. None of them left either. Because they had set the goals and consequences themselves, they accepted them. Even if they did not recall setting those goals, their progress had been communicated daily. It was always right in front of them. They heard it in the huddles and saw it on the communication board. No one could claim they did not know. They took responsibility for their work. I was proud of my team that day. I was even more proud the next year when they had the best outcomes on all of their goals across all of my areas.

The Lesson: What You Need to Know …

Qaalfa: Use emotional response to failure as a diagnostic.
Kalina: It's best if accountability is taken, not given.

We have already learned how important motivation (the personal connection for the employee) and engagement (the relating of the personal motivation with strategic direction) is in cultural transformation. One of the outcomes of engagement is employee effort. The more engaged employees are, the more effort they will expend to make the behavioral change you are seeking. It should be no surprise that not all effort will be productive or successful. You will not always be able to preempt these failure points. It hit Greg when he had experienced so much success that they began to take it for granted. When a member of the team changed, so did the team's success rate. Some of these failure points are more subtle and just warning signs. Rhonda explained how her new team let her down in not participating in an event—an act that signaled disengagement. Little lapses in the transformation will be ever present. Central to overcoming these setbacks is accountability.

There are two classes of accountability: push and pull. Push accountability occurs when an employee has accountability thrust on him or her. This may well feel like a hammer coming down when applied with regularity. Greg described this in the opening chapter when he talked about his earlier leadership style as militaristic, hierarchical, and heavy handed. Back then, Greg would tell you in no uncertain terms what was expected of you and what you were responsible for. Of course, managers have to deliver these sorts of messages on occasion, but a service leader will only need to do so when there is little other option to inspire that same employee. A service leader wants pull accountability: The employee takes ownership on his or her own. Pull accountability leads to faster turnaround times. Pull accountability cannot be legislated. It cannot be imposed; it is initiated by the employee. Engaged employees are much more likely to display pull accountability. Disengaged employees will often need push accountability. Push accountability often leaves those already disengaged feeling like scapegoats and further divorced from the outcomes. This results in poor recovery.

When it is boiled down, accountability is about what happens when there has been a failure of some sort. You rarely hear about accountability when things are running smoothly or above expectations. It is one of the first things managers will want to get straight when there has been a failure. The engaged employee will want to own the problem so he or she can improve. The disengaged employee will feel guilty at best and like a scapegoat at worst. Indeed, you can use the employee's response to failure as a measure of engagement, especially in the early days. We have already stated that the manager will want to monitor things closely in the early days. Under such circumstances, employees can more easily feign engagement for the sake of the boss. We referred to this as a kind of Hawthorne effect.

Managers can determine the true level of an employee's engagement and accountability by the employee's emotional response to failure (big and small). Generally, only engaged employees who have taken ownership will feel even more determined when they hit a roadblock. The cultural transformation is well on its way if most employees feel this way. Greg had faith in his employees and his own judgment of how they would respond when his department did not meet their agreed target. Although they were obviously not pleased, they doubled down on effort in the next year and outperformed most other departments.

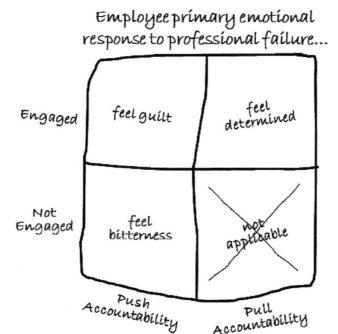

Employee primary emotional
response to professional failure...

Engaged employees who have had accountability forced on them are more likely to feel guilt. They are engaged and thus are motivated to want to help the organization succeed with its strategy but may not yet feel ready to take on ownership. This may be especially prevalent in the early stages when employees' confidence may not yet match their desire to help with the change program. This is when you as a manager will want to push a little, that is, outline responsibilities and expectations. That push should come with the continued engagement work mentioned in the previous chapter. As you push, be prepared for some failures along the way. The trial-and-error behaviors should be encouraged even though it necessarily means that errors, failures, and false starts will occasionally happen. Handling those false starts when you have applied push accountability will mean alleviating feelings of guilt. You will have already minimized these feelings and minimized the length of time they persist if you have been engaging in the engagement actions showing appreciation.

Employees who feel something close to bitterness or even anger in response to a failure tend to be unengaged under push accountability. This is the situation you will find yourself in most often if you have not been conducting the motivation and engagement activities in earnest. If you find your employees in this category too often, you must redouble your motivation and Engagement Bowtie activity and intensify your modeling behavior as a service leader. If you cannot do it yourself, bring someone onboard to help you do it. This is essentially what Greg did when he was looking for a new manager for his department. He did not just look for clinical skill; he knew he needed a certain type of character to balance his leadership style at that time. In his own words from Chapter 2: "Perhaps I needed someone who was good at recognizing and having fun. I had interviewed another candidate who fit that description. She had a great attitude, and service and recognition seemed intuitive to her, but she had absolutely no leadership experience." Greg took a risk here. He was learning that you have to do things differently sometimes if you want different results than you have had in the past. We are all familiar with Einstein's famous definition of "insanity: doing the same thing over and over again and expecting different results."* The brilliance of Greg's move was this new manager would make his natural inclination toward push accountability more effective. He would get two things from this new manager: (1) His employees would get more encouragement because the new manager would naturally perform Engagement Bowtie behavior; and (2) he would get someone he could model besides Rhonda. In other words, he could learn from the new manager's talents. The end result was a speeding up of the transformation.

It becomes clear that the key to accountability in a cultural transformation is engagement. No one likes failure or setback, and even fewer enjoy being called out on it. Accountability is necessary for there to be progress, however. Accountability is that piece of the transformation puzzle that ensures that lessons are not lost along the way. This will help you avoid relearning the same thing repeatedly. To do so, there must be openness about setbacks and consequences. You and the organization must learn what works and what does not. Push accountability without proper engagement will kill your transformation. Engagement is what prevents both the syndrome of burying of heads in the sand and a cycle of bitterness and anger as the inevitable occasional failure occurs as employees attempt different ways of working.

While pull accountability is the ideal, part of the role of a manager will always require a bit of push accountability. When employee efforts have not led to a targeted goal (i.e., failure), it is time to act on accountability. As a manager, you will want employees to be open about it among themselves and with you so that everyone will be free to ask why the results are the way they are and what is needed to change moving forward. Without Engagement Bowtie activities, employees will likely feel that this "open" discussion is a witch hunt for a scapegoat, and they will feel bitter.

There is much less need for a handbook on how to deal with pull accountability. One of the early signs Rhonda saw in Greg was his display of pull accountability. Greg came to Rhonda and asked for help (see Chapter 1, "Begin to Spark"). At that early stage, he was part frustrated, part scared, but mostly determined to succeed. He did not yet know how, but he had set his mind on succeeding. Rhonda saw this spark and fanned it vigorously with Engagement Bowtie activities. Of course, most employees will not display the same characteristics Greg did early on. If they did,

---

* http://www.notable-quotes.com/e/einstein_albert.html

there would be little need for this book. Part of the work of the transformation is to get employees to the point of accepting ownership for change (i.e., pull accountability). Before this happens, you will need to push a bit in that direction. To clear the path and avoid accountability bitterness, try the following:

- **Invoke the Engagement Bowtie** (see Chapter 4, "Connect to Engage").
- **Set concrete goals jointly.** Employees should be involved in the shaping of the Patient Experience targets, and they need to make them concrete. The first important thing here is that goals must be Patient Experience related. This will be a natural by-product if you have been doing your Engagement Bowtie activity. It is not enough to have satisfaction scores that are hospital- (organization-) wide. Each team needs to identify how the team can contribute to the end experience. This also applies to back office operations—admin, legal, human resources (HR), accounting—there may be some degrees of separation, but that does not mean there is no connection. Jointly identify the extent to which the experience is affected and create a goal around bettering it. In that sense, goals need to be concrete. It is not enough to say: "We want highly satisfied patients." You may say: "We want forty-five percent of our patients to give us a score of nine." You may then drill deeper and say: "We want at least ninety percent of employees to smile as they enter a patient's room." The specific ideas will come from the employees.
- **Allow empowerment.** Employees should be able to have the freedom to decide how they will achieve the goals and, if they change their minds or learn better ways, change course. Empowerment is a concept that employees and managers often say they want. Managers are often afraid to allow it, and employees are often afraid to take it. Managers are afraid because they are unsure employees will do the right thing. That is, they do not trust the employees. We described this previously in Chapter 4, "Connect to Engage," when we described one of the benefits of the Engagement Bowtie is that managers begin to gather more and more evidence that their employees are in fact doing the right things. As this happens, managers begin to trust employees and are more willing to empower employees.

  It is often the case that employees do not act empowered when they have been given the authority to be empowered because they in turn are afraid of that potential accountability conversation if things do not turn out as hoped. As the Engagement Bowtie cycle takes hold, employees will begin to see that their efforts are appreciated and feel less likely to be blamed. The Engagement Bowtie activities effectively reduce "CYA"* attitudes among employees, which in turn eliminates vestiges of a blame culture.

---

* CYA refers to "cover your ass," the need to always put oneself in a position that can be defended and not have blame attributed to you. CYA attitudes abound in cultures that seek to attribute blame.

■ **Provide continuous feedback.** Employees should be continuously aware of progress or its lack and the reasons behind this. Each outcome should be tracked back to the activity that led to it. This enables corrective action to be taken. Of course, you will already be doing this if you have invoked the Engagement Bowtie. Part of the Engagement Bowtie involves showing appreciation for employee effort. Also required is feedback on progress or lack thereof. The continuous nature of the feedback you provide will allow for issues to be spotted more quickly. This will mean the corrections required will be and feel less drastic than might be necessary if problems are allowed to fester. Rhonda did this in an informal way when she provided next-to-immediate feedback to her team that true participation at the event she sponsored was necessary. Greg did this more formally with his pushpin board of tracking information.

■ **Utilize the peer-to-peer power.** Peer-to-peer accountability is as important as peer-to-peer appreciation. While it is difficult, if not impossible, to legislate this behavior, you can encourage it. As you are invoking the Engagement Bowtie, pay special attention to instances when an employee holds a colleague accountable. Express appreciation to that employee for what the employee has done. This is another instance of fanning a spark. You will want colleagues to learn that this is exactly the sort of behavior you seek. An offshoot result is that employees will come to expect to hear and value it from colleagues. When employees realize that they are not being blamed but rather helped to succeed, they will be maximally inclined to display pull accountability.

Encouraging peer-to-peer accountability should be done by giving employees a quick way of signaling their colleagues that their actions need attention. It is best if this can be done from a distance (e.g., from across the hall), nonverbally, and immediately. Rhonda's take on this is the "red/blue card" idea. Everyone at Community General must wear ID cards. Issued along with the ID cards is a separate study/job aid card that is red on one side and blue on the other. When an employee sees another doing something that could be improved, the observer employee can discreetly show the red side of the card to the employee. This alerts the offending employee that he or she needs to reconsider whatever it is that he or she is doing. It will usually spark a chat later. Sometimes, that chat will be, "Thanks, I changed course"; at other times, it will be, "Why did you show me the red card?" The red card situation can also be fodder at a team meeting; the team can revisit that situation and develop better ways of dealing with it. When you do red card someone, think through the situation. Be sure that the employee you identify has not been forced into making the best of bad choices because of decisions made elsewhere. In fact, some of your greatest success will be had by identifying upstream causes to problems.

Of course, as with the nurse who stated in no uncertain terms she was not going to change, it may sometimes be necessary to surgically remove that cancer to the culture you are trying to transform. You will immediately recognize these employees because they self-identify right up front and actively, even proudly, display their resistance. You are unlikely to motivate or engage them. If you have tried repeatedly but you have failed, you will of course see no effort from that employee to help in the transformation. You then have a choice: keep the person around or get rid of the individual. If in your assessment they cannot be brought around and their influence is greater than their contribution, eliminate them from your culture. If they are not putting in the effort with respect to the cultural transformation but they make a contribution elsewhere *and* their cultural influence is negligible, keep them around until you can bring in a replacement who contributes both operationally and culturally. Consider this a last-ditch effort. Remember, Greg was not shown the door immediately. He was given a bit of push accountability and provided with encouragement via Rhonda.

Chapter 6

Succeed, Then Recognize

Rhonda: Recognition—marinate in it, don't just sprinkle.

We had come so far in the transition of our culture. We had found our motivation and helped as others found theirs. We had engaged the employees through open, transparent, and adult-to-adult communication, and the employees were not only accepting consistency and accountability but were craving it. The outcomes were being reached. We had achieved great success across the strategies. Doctors were starting to compliment us, patients were telling stories of how it had changed from their previous visits, and money was starting to be there to invest in the growth of our business. The most satisfying outcome of the change was the sense of pride we felt when we were out in the community. It was always a little daunting when you were at your kid's soccer game and someone approached you, asking: "Don't you work at the hospital?" In the past, you never knew what they were going to say about their experience. That was changing rapidly with our successes. Now, you felt confident that they were going to tell a great story. Even if they did not, you could tell them with assurance that any problems would be taken care of. You also felt a sense of unity toward the goals.

Since there was so much success, there were many more opportunities to recognize the people creating the success. I know saying "thank you" should be intuitive, but for everyone, it does not come naturally. I bought 2,000 thank you cards and was determined that they were going to be used. I started by placing a package on each of the desks in the administrative suite. Getting the administrators to complete the cards was easy. Most of them were really good about saying thank you. The managers were good about it, too. The managers found out I had the thank you cards, and they were approaching me asking for them. Half of the work was done. We needed to know they were writing them as well. In the hallways and work areas, you could overhear employees talking about receiving the cards. Now that administration and management were writing thank you cards, the last groups to focus on were at the director level and the front line thanking their peers.

At one of the director meetings, I passed out a thank you card to each director. I asked them to imagine that their best employee was being recruited by the hospital up the street. How would they feel if they lost that person to the competitor? What kind of deficit would they feel? What kind of advantage would that give the competition? Through the discussion, we concluded that many people who leave do so because they do not feel appreciated, and during recruitment efforts the potential candidate is made to feel important. I told them that card represented their chance to rerecruit their top talent and perhaps save them from becoming a former employee. In the card, they were asked to address that employee by name, thank them, and mention specifically what made them special and valuable. The card was to be concluded with a sentence letting the employee know if they were given the chance they would hire them all over again, and that they were the standard all other candidates were compared to. A few years later, I was talking to the CFO [chief financial officer]. He shared that completing that exercise taught him a lot about what his most important role as a leader is. Leaders do not do the tasks; they make sure competent, compassionate people are there to do them.

I got my first employee satisfaction results. I knew without a doubt they would be stellar. That group walked the halls with their heads held high and filled with their accomplishments. Our patient satisfaction scores were great, too. When we got our employee engagement results, our department was one of the best in the hospital. Of course, as usual, Greg gave me a run for the money, and his results were higher. Barely higher, but higher! Imagine my surprise when I learned that my area of focus (the lowest score I got) was in regard to the question that asked the employees if they felt recognized recently for doing good work. This was going to take some investigation to find out what caused this gap between my reality and the reality of my team.

Just like with the patient satisfaction, if you want to know what someone is thinking, ask the source directly. So, that is just what I did. I found out that the department really did not revolve around only me. There were some people who felt I did a great job recognizing them, but they were not sure anyone outside our department knew how well they did. There was a story one of them told about a new process she had been trying to master. She had worked for days on this new skill. Although she had practiced and was fully engaged, she had not gotten it right. Well, one day she was faced with the task at hand. When she accomplished it, she was so excited for her success. She said she came to my office to tell me, and she was completely deflated to find I was not there. She next went to see the managers, and they were not there either. She had one of the most accomplished moments of her career and no one to share it with. I could not believe how blind I had been. I had taken all of the responsibility for recognition while I expected (demanded really) peer accountability.

The next day at our huddles, I changed the course of action. We went through the information that needed to be communicated. Afterward, we went around the circle. Each employee had to thank another employee for something they had seen them do the day before. It did not take long for that to spread through our department like wildfire. Soon, they were recognizing each other consistently. I also started sending the CEO [chief executive officer] a list every Friday of thank you cards that I was requesting him to send. Now, the recognition was coming from all levels.

On a hospital and department basis, the recognition was gaining consistency. The final thought of each Daily Huddle was reserved for the team to recognize a peer for working on wonderful (wow). Some days, it seemed like pulling teeth to get the employees to recognize each other. Before long, though, the appreciation was flowing from person to person. Just like with everything else, people like choices. Some people preferred to recognize people publicly. We even had instances of people going to other department's huddles to thank an employee. There were also those who preferred to put the recognition in writing. We offered a paper thank you card as well as an electronic version. The paper card could be left in a box to be distributed to the employee mentioned. In the electronic version, the employees could click a tab on the intranet, choose the employee's name, and write out the text of the thank you. The manager and employee would receive the card by e-mail. The first month, there were less than fifty of the combined cards completed. Within six months, that number had grown to more than 500. Almost four years later, the number is still in excess of 500. The e-mailed stories of people going above and beyond did not stop either. There were still several a day being sent out. Some of the cards were thanking an employee for helping a team member out, and some involved outstanding patient care; as various as the senders were the reasons for the wows. The doctors even jumped onboard and starting recognizing the employees for the work they were doing.

By this time, I had figured out if I wanted to make something stick, measurement was the glue. We had a lot of cultural things in place around appreciation, but nothing was formal. Informal appreciation, as good as it feels, sometimes goes by the wayside when other things take priority. Things that are not measured do not continue. I had to take something as intangible as appreciation and figure out a way to measure it without the measurement being noticeable or feeling like a precursor to laying blame. This was bigger task than I alone was ready to handle. I needed to go see Greg.

Greg: Appreciation is not recognition.

As we began seeing all of our success, I felt this real need to say thank you. I wanted to make sure the staff knew that the great things that were happening were because of them. Rhonda sends out "wows" that a lot of time looked to me like she was thanking them for just doing their job. I talked to her about it, and she giggled and said, "Well yeah; don't you want people at work to do their jobs? Imagine how much we could get done if everyone worked while they were on duty." That was a whole new way of thinking for me. Not long ago, I would not even say "Hi" when I passed by employees in the hallway, much less recognize them for efforts that I expected and that they were getting paid for. I thought as the director my time was supposed to be spent taking care of issues when something went wrong. One day in a directors' meeting, Rhonda passed out a bundle of thank you cards and told us to think of someone in our departments who had done something well. She then taught us how to write a thank you card. It dawned on me that I had not done it before because it did not come easy to me. Prior to that five-minute exercise, I would have simply stared at the blank card and wondered what to write.

At the next meeting, one of the other directors reported that an employee who she sent one of the thank you cards to came to her that afternoon. The employee thanked her for the card and said in all of the years she had worked here no one had ever said thanks. Sure, management had passed out gifts during the holidays and hospital week. The employee considered this holiday gift giving as pretty generic, though. The difference with the thank you card is that it specifically mentioned what she had contributed. That employee was thinking about leaving the hospital, but this simple act got her to see things differently. She began to become engaged. We would have lost a good employee except for something as simple as saying, "I appreciate you." So, I started to say thank you. I even encouraged them to say thank you to each other. If I learned of a colleague thanking another, I showed appreciation for that, too. Rhonda told me that during her goal-setting session with her own team, they even made saying thank you one of their measurable goals.

Rhonda and her team had also developed some ways to track patient and employee compliments in a central database. There were cards (both paper and electronic) that could be filled out, and of course there were the wows that she collected through e-mail. Employee comments were also tracked. Everything was put into this database.

I could see that some of my employees had over fifty compliments, and while I had said thank you, their peers and patients had said thank you, there was still something missing. We needed to get that behavior to spread to all of our team members and throughout the entire hospital. How could we spotlight those employees that were being complimented over and over again?

Rhonda and I had talked about a formal program for dealing with the compliments we were tracking. Luckily, our system had a database, and so that was the easy part. The hard part was always what to do with the information that we had tracked. A team of us came up with the idea of a monthly celebration to reward those that had been mentioned more than ten times by peers, physicians, and patients. We gave those that met these criteria shirts that identified them as top performers for satisfaction. We allowed and encouraged them to wear the shirts on Fridays. Our goal was to have everyone wanting a shirt. By the end of that year, fifty percent of our team hospital-wide was proudly sporting one of those shirts on Fridays!

As our culture became one where recognition for success was the norm, consistency and fairness became very important. In our formal celebration, we created a tiered program. Ten compliments equaled a free shirt; fifteen got a lunch kit to go along with the shirt, and so on. Our top performers got a certificate to display in their department for their patients and colleagues to see.

Just as I was learning what recognition was, I was learning what recognition wasn't. For example, you cannot promise the moon or have a contest to dole out recognition. If you give one performer a big budget-busting (e.g., $3,000) reward, you won't have anything left for the rest of the group. If team members believe that only the absolute top performer will be recognized, they will not even strive to be in the top ten. You also have to recognize performance across the different departments. Hospitals have historically put a lot of importance around the results for the clinical core measures. These are the steps that are proven to drive the best clinical outcomes. If hospitals put all of their recognition efforts around individual core measure performance, anyone outside of nursing is not eligible to be recognized. Recognition has to be available for everyone but should be earned. One thing that was intuitive to me but I had to help my peers like Rhonda understand was that if you recognize employees when they do not actually meet the goal, then you will get a team that feels entitled even when performance is absent.

Recognition cannot be used like a shotgun. You cannot pass out a branded beach towel during hospital week or serve a fancy meal during the holidays and consider that recognition. Although it is appreciation, it is not recognition unless it is for a specific act. If you want the employee to do a specific thing again, you thank them for the specific thing they did.

The Lesson: What You Need to Know ...

Qaalfa: Appreciate effort, recognize success.
Kalina: Appreciation builds engagement, while recognition builds performance.

In Chapter 2, "Personalize to Motivate," we spoke about tapping into employees' values and emotions to get them excited about their job from a personal point of view. In Chapter 4, "Connect to Engage," we saw that showing employees appreciation for their effort is essential to building devoted and proactive employees. Appreciation is used to give employees a sense of honor and dignity. It should be given for the honest effort employees give on a daily basis to do the activities that comprise their job in a customer-centric way. You should be able to tell a story of how each job group has an impact on the Customer Experience and identify when employees put real effort into behaviors that the cultural transformation requires. In Chapter 5, "Fail, then Account," we learned that ownership of the change comes in two forms: active and passive. While active accountability is most desirable, passive accountability is also necessary to push things along even when employees' confidence may not yet be fully functioning. In other words, accountability prepares us for a course of action when things do not turn out as hoped. It gives us a backdrop from which our learning can spring. Recognition is the opposite side of the coin from accountability. When employees do the things the cultural transformation requires successfully, recognition is the order of the day.

A recognition system is to the cultural transformation what oxygenated blood is to muscle. It pertains to all parts of the organization and brings them nutrients to keep them active and functioning. Recognition is an important subcategory of appreciation that forms part of the Engagement Bowtie. While appreciation is used nonsparingly for engaged effort regardless of whether success is seen at that point in time, recognition is best reserved for specific efforts that have resulted in success. Greg was clear on this point of view. Rhonda was so embedded in the Engagement Bowtie activities that she failed to distinguish the recognition. Greg knew he needed to make the appreciation-recognition distinction.

Recognition is a way of reinforcing the activities that have proven to be effective because they have already resulted in success for the organization's strategy (e.g., Patient Experience in the case of Community General). In other words, it is about reinforcing good performance. As Greg put it: "One thing that was intuitive to me but I had to help my peers like Rhonda understand was that if you recognize employees when they do not actually meet the goal, then you will get a team that feels entitled even when performance is absent." For a true cultural transformation, both appreciation and recognition are needed. Appreciation builds engagement, and recognition builds performance.

There are two ways of recognizing employees: formal and informal. To achieve cultural transformation, informal recognition should precede formal and then continue in parallel to it. Starting formal recognition without informal to support it will lead to skepticism as employees may not be ready to receive praise. It is interesting to think that even formal praise can be detrimental if used inappropriately. A common effect of inappropriately applied formal recognition programs is employee cynicism. In organizations where formal recognition exists but where informal recognition does not to any large extent, recognition itself may be derided among employees, or it is taken as a joke. Often, it is embarrassing for many employees to be recognized publicly in such schemes even when the employee may be inwardly proud of the accomplishment. This embarrassment we speak of stems squarely from being associated with a program so awkwardly maligned by peers, not the embarrassment some employees feel at having the public spotlight shown on them.

Informal recognition refers to the innumerable ways in which supervisors can demonstrate their appreciation of a job well done. Informal recognition focuses on

spontaneous, sincere, and personal appreciation of an employee's successful efforts.*
These are good not only for improving performance but also for boosting morale.
This recognition also encourages coworkers to informally reward each other, doing
the job for you in essence.† This last bit is the mark of the positive peer pressure
mentioned previously. Indeed, take it as a sign that cultural transformation is pro-
gressing at a healthy pace if you begin to see coworkers step outside of their normal
comfort zone to recognize each other for behavior aligned with Patient Experience.

The key task will be to identify the types of attitude, thinking, and behavior
that should be rewarded. More important, you will need to make it applicable to
front and back office individuals, employees and management.

The first thing to do is to identify the behaviors that you will be informally
recognizing:

- See the patients' experience from their perspective to understand the emotional experience, the subtle clues, and the psychological journey your
patients have (remember Chapter 2, "Personalize to Motivate"). This will
allow you to begin to understand some of the little things that are central to
Patient Experience but that may be overlooked in formal job specifications
of employees.
- Identify desired Patient Experience practices and make sure employees
have a solid idea of what these behaviors are. In Chapter 4, "Connect to
Engage," we asked you to create stories that tie every employees' work to
the Patient Experience.
  - It is important that employees see that everyone is included (management,
  cleaners, security, physicians, etc.). This helps prevent the recognition
  from becoming something that is only for those lower in the organization.
- Actively look for behaviors that support the Customer Experience transformation, which in Chapter 4 we referred to as active listening.

An example of informal recognition was when the CEO read the patient compliment letter out loud and congratulated the named specific employees for their
success. Informal recognition has the following characteristics:

- It relates to good performance or success (in this case, patient satisfaction).
- It feels spontaneous.
- It comes from a highly regarded influencer (someone whose opinion matters
to the employee).

---

* Michigan State University, Informal rewards. http://www.hr.msu.edu/recognition/informal-
Rewards.htm (accessed November 2012).
† For a useful list of some informal reward tactics, see http://www.successfactors.com/articles/
rewarding-talent/.

■ It is related to a specific named action. The specificity is required because you will want the word to spread among employees regarding the exact reason for the recognition. This is where the learning takes place. Without stating the specific action that led to the success, all that employees are left with is who received the accolade. If the person does not match their already-formed opinion, strong political undercurrents may start forming. To avoid these currents, be clear on the specific successful action that led to the kudos and be transparent with all employees.

Let us take a closer look at each of these elements of informal recognition. Like all recognition *informal recognition should relate to good performance* (success). Recognition is different from appreciation, which is done for effort. Recognition (formal and informal) should be tied to success to embed the message "this is what works in this organization." But, beware: a common mistake often is to recognize only grand successes. You should informally recognize the more mundane but successful behaviors. Employees should learn what success looks like and how it can be achieved through your recognition efforts. They should feel that they are potential recognition candidates for the successes they achieve as defined by the organization. While recognition stories often revolve around weird and wonderful extraordinarily high performance, it is the mundane replicable successes that will build culture. Do not look for the extraordinary; look for the good. Use informal recognition to reinforce the success seen in the business-as-usual environment. Use formal recognition for more grand examples of success.

Informal recognition should feel spontaneous. This makes it look genuine, and it allows for greater frequency. This tone of spontaneity also usually implies that it takes little time to deliver. If managers approach informal recognition as a scheduled activity, it will be perceived by employees as just a tick-box exercise, a task and obligation, rather than honest sincere kudos. As a manager, you will need to convince your staff that you genuinely care and are happy about their success, even the small successes. You could make a stop in the hallway to say thanks for a job especially well done. The example of the CEO reading the letter felt spontaneous even though it took time to gather the employees. The fact that it was the CEO no doubt helped employees walk away from it understanding that this was meaningful and sincere and a meaningful use of their time.

Informal recognition most often occurs in the natural working environment of the employees and, if possible, just within earshot of others. Making informal recognition public is another way of enhancing its effect, and it allows for others to hear and learn what recognition is given for. This does not mean you will need to organize public gatherings and copy everyone in on each e-mail. It simply means to do the informal recognizing in such a way it encourages others to ask about it, to wonder why someone received accolades. As you will be modeling the behavior, peers will learn that there is not a specific time for recognition—any time is a good informal recognition time.

Informal recognition comes from a highly regarded influencer (someone whose opinion matters to the employee). This is often a person in a position of authority like the CEO at Community General. Beware: many people in positions of authority are not highly regarded by employees. Recognition by these figureheads tends not to be very effective for cultural transformation and can lead to the cynicism mentioned previously. In the beginning of a transformation, influencers can be those who are most resistant to the change. In such cases, you will have to double your Engagement Bowtie efforts but at the same time employ some push accountability. If your role does not have enough formal authority (stick) to back up the push accountability, consider the cultural transformation dead unless you can get a person who does have that authority to back you up. Most often, however, you will find your motivation and engagement efforts will have created a couple of meaningful sparks in the organization. You will then use those people in the same way Rhonda relied on Greg's influence and standing with employees when she was still considered an outsider.

The goal should be to have colleagues show each other informal recognition (i.e., peer-to-peer recognition). As Rhonda put it, one of her employees "had one of the most accomplished moments of her career and no one to share it with. I could not believe how blind I had been. I had taken all of the responsibility for recognition while I expected (demanded really) peer accountability." Peer-to-peer informal recognition requires that employees are (1) aware of what the desired behaviors are and (2) care and see the goal as a shared responsibility. For some employees, recognizing peers will come naturally. Others will require coaching. The organization, however, needs to encourage it and create the space and conditions for it to exist. Those conditions are motivation, modeling, and engagement. Informal recognition needs to become a way of communicating, not something a few in the organization do.

Informal recognition is related to a specific named action. The specificity is required because you will want the word to spread among employees regarding the exact reason for the recognition. This is where the learning takes place. Without stating the specific action that led to the success, all that employees are left with is who received the accolade. If the person does not match their already-formed opinion, strong political undercurrents may start forming. To avoid these currents, be clear on the specific successful action that led to the kudos and be transparent with all employees.

It goes without saying that to recognize the behavior one must be able to spot it in the first place, as outlined previously. This is not as easy as it seems at first. It does not come naturally to most people. If you went around your organization asking employees to list a number of patient-centric activities, rarely would you hear anyone list the janitor's cleaning standard. This is why you as the cultural transformation agent will need to identify the stories that show how everyone affects the Patient Experience. After that, it is only a matter of pointing out and recognizing those successes.

Rhonda and Greg consistently implemented their huddles, team meetings, and other recognition activities and appreciation gestures such that they always related a specific behavior to a success (recognition) or failure (accountability). Furthermore, while giving recognition, there is need to indicate (especially in the beginning) how that action benefits the Patient Experience (the goal). This was previously described as part of the Engagement Bowtie set of activities. For example, a stop in the hall to informally recognize the janitor's work should not simply stop with a "Good job, Tom." Instead, make it specific and in the best case describe the impact it has on the overall goal: "Those floors are spotless, Tom; patients will feel at home. This is why we get tens on our cleanliness ratings. Thank you."

We put a lot of emphasis on the informal recognition because it is commonly overlooked and neglected in transformation programs. In addition, the human resources function of most organizations will generally have some sort of expertise at setting up formal recognition programs. A quick Internet search on recognition programs will point you in the direction of a number of resources on formal recognition schemes. The vast resources out there do a great job of presenting various methods of setting up a successful formal recognition program. Nevertheless, formal recognition programs play an important role. As Rhonda put it: "We had a lot of cultural things in place around appreciation, but nothing was formal. Informal appreciation, as good as it feels, sometimes goes by the wayside when other things take priority."

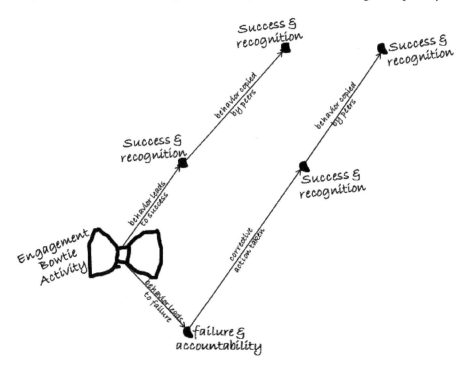

Recognition (informal and formal) serves to magnify proven behavior leading to success. In a similar light, accountability is there to help ensure successful corrective action, and learning takes place when a failure occurs. The relationship between engagement, accountability, and recognition can be summed in the following diagram. Engagement will lead to employees putting in the effort to make the change. When that effort leads to success, recognition should be the result on occasion. When that effort leads to failure, accountability will allow for effective corrective action to be taken. When this corrective action produces results, recognition will kick in to highlight the success and help get others to model that behavior.

Chapter 7

Inject Fun to Release Pressure

Rhonda: Have fun while figuring out what fun means.

I was a teenager in the eighties, so I was fully subscribed to Cyndi Lauper's philosophy that we all just want to have fun. Working in healthcare is the most satisfying career one can have, but face it, it is work. There are things that are frustrating, scary, sad, and mundane. In developing this culture, we had concentrated on motivation, servant leadership, employee engagement and development, accountability, and recognition. It was becoming a well-rounded culture. You could see the improvements reflected in the expressions on the faces of those you passed in the hallway. It just wasn't complete yet. We were working hard together; shouldn't we play hard together, too? All work and no play make for a very dull existence, right? So, we would play together and have fun, but it would be fun with a purpose. It amazed me that not everyone wanted to have fun together. When I mentioned fun sometimes, it was like I had said we were going to do something bad. It had never occurred to me that I would have to mandate fun!

It has to start somewhere, so I started with my department. Timing was perfect. Each year there is a week to celebrate the Business Office employees. It is typically just a routine celebration of cake and punch with an insignificant branded gift to commemorate the appreciation. I saw an opportunity to do something big this year! Business Office Week was coming up the next month. At the huddle, I asked the team how they would like to celebrate. I was made aware that in years past all patient access team members received a gift from the system with a tray of cookies. I agreed with them that gifts are nice, but I challenged them on what we could do to have fun together. One of them sarcastically said, "We could all go on a cruise together." Well, they may not want to take on the challenge, but I am always up for one. I was going to take my entire department on a cruise without ever leaving dry ground and for under a thousand dollars!

I called the managers and team leads together, and we brainstormed how we could all go on a cruise during our celebration week. As usual, they all looked at me like I was insane, but I never let that stop me. Before the hour was over, we had planned our cruise and divided the work. Our hospital had a quarterly award that was given to the department that had evolved a practice to lead to a new way of achieving greatness. In the previous quarter, we won that award for our ability to collect more money while improving our patient satisfaction. The award came with a thousand dollars to spend. So, with money to spend and an itinerary planned, we would set sail to celebrate. On Monday, we would leave port and head to Mexico, where we enjoyed a bon voyage buffet and took photos of everyone as the ship set sail. The following day would be spent at sea, so we would have gambling tables. We found really inexpensive blackjack and roulette table toppers. Everyone came down, and we served them alcohol-free cocktails while they played the tables. We had cards and dice to even it out. The team was having a blast. On another day at sea, we painted porcelain pieces that we could keep on our desk as a reminder of our weeklong working vacation. We all put our fingerprints on a platter to hang on the wall. It represented all of our touches in creating the new us. We also docked in Italy, where we had chair massages and smoothies. On our final day, we anchored in New Orleans. The team decorated carts, chairs, and even themselves as floats, and we took our Mardi Gras parade through the adjoining departments.

It was time to spread the fun through the hospital. If within our departments the relationships were strengthening due to the fun, it would definitely help interdepartmental relationships. We started the fun with hospital Olympics during hospital week. Each department entered a team, dressed in their team uniform, and competed in events like bed- and tray-making races, bedpan toss across, and personal protective equipment relays. Much to my surprise, not every department was a happy participant in the fun. That was true even in my own department. Even though they had fun together, they did not want to branch outside of our departmental events. I believe, though, that even those that pretend they do not want to have fun really do want to, but they just need a little push. So, this is where the accountability comes in; I would just make everyone participate in the fun. After making them for the first few times, they really began to like doing it. That year, we also had a hospital-wide chili cook-off and a carnival to celebrate receiving an award for quality. With each event, more and more departments and more employees participated. People began looking forward to the events.

The fun was extending past the special events and into the daily functions. We looked for reasons to have fun together. A birthday or anniversary was never forgotten. It was little things, but they were still fun. You also saw people become more jovial in their work interactions.

Greg: You will have fun, dammit.

To help our team with their development, we read books together and had discussion around them. One of the books that we read talked about mandatory fun. Every time the hospital had an event, whether it was as big as a chili cook-off or as routine as a Daily Huddle, we were there. Rhonda had set her team straight on the first day in her department that participation and fun were mandatory. About six months in of her telling them fun is mandatory, the hospital was raising money for an employee campaign. One of the fundraisers was a dunking booth where employees could pay to dunk their leaders into a tank of water. As Rhonda's team watched her go into the tank, they yelled in unison, "Fun is mandatory."

When I was in the military, I had this job that I hated. I did not just dislike it. Literally, I could feel myself getting physically ill as I got close to work each morning. I can remember what that felt like so vividly. In the past few months, I had really started to care about the people I work with and never wanted any of them to feel that way. We were becoming a very successful team. Everyone was working hard. The culture was becoming so real, we could feel it. I wanted everyone to really enjoy coming to work—we needed to have fun together. I thought back to the jobs that I really enjoyed, and it was obvious that the jobs I enjoyed the most were the ones where I had fun with my coworkers. In many of the situations, we had fun together on and off the job. I really knew those people and could count on them if I needed help. Isn't that what we need at work as well: a group of people who really care about each other and do not want to fail because they don't want to let each other down? We had accountability, but that makes people do it right because they do not want the negative consequences. What would it look like if everyone were pushing it to the limit because they cared about the team?

I met with my team leads and manager. We discussed where we were as a team, and it was evident that there were pockets of people within the department that were friends and had fun together. I wanted to give the entire team an opportunity to have fun together outside of work. The weather was getting nice out, and there was a nice park less than five miles from the hospital. I wanted to have a departmental picnic. In that first meeting, I discovered that some of the team leads did not necessarily want to get together and have fun. As we learned in the other things we were doing, the team would follow their lead. I talked to the departmental leadership and told them straight up they were required to participate. Even if it were only the leadership that showed up, we would all be there. I knew that would not happen, though. If I was making the leaders come, they would get their team there. After a little planning on their part and a lot of setup on mine, we had what was to be the first of a biannual departmental get-together.

That first picnic was a bigger success than I ever imagined it would be. Everyone had a great time. We got to meet each other's families. We all played a role. Several of us cooked the burgers and hot dogs, while others set up the games and the rest of the food. Everyone enjoyed the meal and playing together. The kids were in the spirit, too. They soon found new friends and discovered what they had in common. When we returned to work the following Monday, the members of the team were different together. Now, they were more invested in each other. They knew their families and what they looked like outside of the maroon scrubs. This fun stuff wasn't fluff; it was real substance. The picnics led to other fun events. Almost monthly, we have a happy hour celebrating something, and once a year I host an appreciation night for my team leads. It is usually a get-together at my house, but most recently we all went out to dinner together.

After four years of picnics and other events, fun has become a cherished part of our culture. The planning starts way in advance, and everyone participates. We often have people come that no longer even work for the hospital. In one of our more recent picnics, one of our team leads that had accepted a promotion in our system joined us. She loved her new job and was grateful for the promotion, but she came back because she missed the people she had worked with. We had come full circle in our culture; we had a nice balance of accountability and recognition held together with a large helping of fun.

The Lesson: What You Need to Know ...

Qaalfa: Put polka dots on that bowtie.
Kalina: Keep it interesting.

We sometimes get pushback at mentioning fun in Patient Experience or any Customer Experience that is not directly related to entertainment. The basis for that sort of thinking in hospitals often stems from the idea that patients are different from customers. Normally, people think of the Patient Experience as involving suffering. On the other hand, great Customer Experiences are often described in Disneyesque terms. Great Customer Experiences are about consistency and deliberate delivery, and that applies to Patient and Customer Experience. Fun is just an enabler of a culture that breeds Customer Experience excellence.

Rhonda and Greg used fun as a vaccine against program sterility and staleness. They injected fun into activities to provide a contrast against work as usual. As Rhonda stated: "Working in healthcare is the most satisfying career one can have, but face it, it is work. There are things that are frustrating, scary, sad, and mundane." To be more precise, work is work without the added stress of having to try doing things differently as is required in a transformation. Work is stressful, and that is basically why it is not play. Work plus transformation is double stress. Fun is used to decrease the stress. Like everything, fun can simply be random, unrelated acts that bring enjoyment, or it can be used to serve a function in your engagement activities (refer to the Engagement Bowtie).

Fun does not have to be wacky. It can simply be different from the norm of the work environment. It is a pressure valve. As you initiate your motivation and engagement activities while maintaining accountability, pressure will build. However, it will not be unbearable pressure if you have applied the drip-feed approach, by which all of the transformation Engagement Bowtie activities are continuous. One of the consequences you will want to be on the lookout for is the slow buildup of pressure. A properly applied Engagement Bowtie will make the pressure a tasteless, odorless gas. You will simply have to open the valve occasionally even when it does not look like it is necessary. The buildup maybe so gradual that employees are not fully aware of the pressure they are under. A key function of the fun valve is to release that pressure.

Another way to think about fun is that it is akin to the movie day at school when the teacher brought in the projector. It was always a day to look forward to even if the content of the film was part of the lesson. It provided a change of pace.

Injecting fun is also a channel for creativity. Nurturing professional creativity is beneficial in getting employees to think of different ways of doing their jobs. After all, the point of the transformation is to get employees to approach their jobs differently. You actually want them to do their job differently—in a way that is aligned with the Patient Experience transformation. Literally demonstrating that in the ways you interact with employees will be beneficial.

So, how do you place a fun valve on some of your Engagement Bowtie activities?

Engagement Bowtie
With "fun" polka dots

- Involve employees in the design and delivery of the fun. Early on, take some cynical comment and transform it into something useful. This is exactly what Rhonda did when one of her employees snidely suggested that the team take a cruise together. It is not only the destination but also the journey that made the trip worthwhile in this instance. Preparing for a fun activity allows for all the creativity, laughs, and excitement to occur. Rhonda injected fun into the Business Office Week preparation. This showed the team that there are different ways of approaching things. Involving employees in the design also ensures that the activity is tailored to the team it is meant for.

■ Do "fun" on a regular basis. You should have predicted we were going to suggest this by now, especially since we are injecting fun into our Engagement Bowtie activities. Like appreciation, motivation, accountability and recognition, and bathing, you want to do it regularly. Injecting fun into your Engagement Bowtie will be like placing polka dots on it. The bowtie is the main item, but fun gives it a bit of style. One of the key issues with grand annual celebrations is that they are rare and infrequent enough to reap the benefits of the fun valve. They are seen as a tick-box exercise. As with informal recognition, the less frequently done, the less genuine it feels. Find a way to bring fun in on a monthly basis and treat it as if it is the first time.

■ Be creative and change it up. The first time you inject fun, it will be in contrast to the way you traditionally do things. If you were to use that same fun injection each time in the future, it simply would become the new tradition. Greg started with the team picnic, but over the next four years fun was injected into many other activities. You may of course repeat a fun activity, but it is best to have it in a mix of fun activities. Following the first bullet point will help you keep full of fun idea variations. Note that fun does not have to mean wacky, extreme, or weird, but it does need to feel different from work as usual.

Greg, true to his natural form, said to his team early on: "You will have fun, dammit." It is true people cannot be ordered to have fun in the regular sense of the word. However, we have defined fun as an activity that cuts across the grain of regular working practices. It is possible to command people to participate. Greg needed to do this with his fun activities at first as they were still in the mental space of the traditional way of working. Greg forced participation. This forced participation would fail miserably if Greg had not also begun wearing his Engagement Bowtie, and even then it took some time for the employees' mindset to adjust. Engagement is crucial to *not* reinforce employees' cynicism. Employees do respond with repeated exposure.

Ultimately, the real benefit of incorporating fun into work is that you, as the leader of change, are actually practicing service leadership (remember Chapter 3, "Serve to Lead"). Putting in the effort to provide enjoyment for your employees outside work shows that you care about them as human beings, about their needs, and in the end is that not what you are asking them to do for your customers? Fun is a universal need and an effective way of bettering your employees' experience.

There is a ton of literature around fun, and we do not attempt to cover all grounds. However, having seen its role in Community General, we did want to emphasize its importance by dedicating a chapter to it.

Fun is commonly evoked in organizations known to have achieved customer experience-oriented excellence. Zappos,* the online shoe retailer, is one of those companies. Their take on fun sounds like this:

> We want just a touch of weirdness to make life more interesting and fun for everyone. ... One of the side effects of encouraging weirdness is that it encourages people to think outside the box and be more innovative. When you combine a little weirdness with making sure everyone is also having fun at work, it ends up being a win-win for everyone: Employees are more engaged in the work that they do, and the company as a whole becomes more innovative.

Another example is Southwest Airlines. They state that to promulgate their "Fun Luving Attitude,"† the following are required:

- Have fun
- Don't take yourself too seriously
- Maintain perspective
- Celebrate successes
- Enjoy your work
- Be a passionate team player

We understand the difference between a hospital, a retailer, and an airline. The point here is to use fun injections to better enable your transformation efforts. These companies successfully live the cultures that have powered them to success, and they each use fun as a tool. We recommend you do the same.

---

* http://about.zappos.com/our-unique-culture/zappos-core-values/create-fun-and-little-weidness
† Southwest Airlines Web site http://www.southwest.com/html/about-southwest/careers/culture.html (accessed November 2012).

Chapter 8

Measure to Coach

Greg: Look behind the numbers.

Through a lot of work, we had the cultural foundation in our department and throughout the hospital that was resulting in success. Now that we had reached success, it was time to lay back and reap the benefits of our labor, or so I thought. I will never forget the day I learned that even a culture purposely created can turn back without the proper discipline. My department had been in the ninety-ninth percentile for patient satisfaction for thirteen months straight. I knew my department was a well-oiled machine, and I no longer had to spend my time looking at the surveys. One day as I was relaxed in my workflow, I received the report of our scores. To my amazement, our scores were all red! Not only had we slipped out of the ninety-ninth percentile, but also we had slipped down below the midpoint. The thing most alarming to me was I did not know why. I realized it had been weeks, months even, since I had looked at a survey or even observed patient interactions with my employees. Since I lead by example, my manager had not been looking at them either. Rhonda always said that measurement was the glue that made it all stick. Well, we had measurement in a sense. We had our results. We had the numbers, but I had to take a deeper look at where the numbers were coming from. I was learning that measurement is much more than reporting numbers or outcomes—it is compliance to behavior standards and outcomes that count. I also had to understand the actions that create the numbers. Sometimes, it is not just the actions you expect to be going on. If there is no compliance with the behavioral standards in place but you are unaware of that, you may be tricked into thinking that you have the wrong behavioral standards in place. So, I sprang into action; in fact, I wound the spring so tightly I began to overmeasure.

Measuring things became an obsession for me. I tracked everything and prided myself that we had more than twenty goals for our team. All of this measuring took a lot of energy and time. I was robbing my team of the energy needed to make improvements and to grow and develop. I was shell-shocked when I was caught off guard with my patient satisfaction drop. I did not like that feeling at all. I never wanted to get caught off guard again, so I was determined to know every number possible.

My CEO [chief executive officer] had gained confidence in me. Funny, with the confidence and recognition of my efforts came his investment in me. I had shown him I was all in, so he started giving me opportunities in return. Our system offered a leadership development program. Since we are a big system and there were a limited number of spots in this course, it was quite an honor to be chosen to attend. In the class, each of us was asked to pick a project for improvement. I picked a hot topic item around safety. There was a lot of attention to safety, and I knew this would let the big guys know I cared about it. I did not choose it because I understood where we were on it or even if we had a need to improve. I went into it for the wrong reasons. I wanted to show the big guys I was aligned with them when I really should have been showing my team that patient safety was at the front of all of my efforts. This was another example of my engagement. I had started doing all that I could to be successful in the areas the system considered important. The problem was I had started doing it for the system and for my own status in the company; I had to do it for the patient. After this exercise in development, I learned that about myself, so I was able to change my purpose. It also allowed me to see that all of my team was not aligned with the purpose of doing it for the patient. I was always learning during this time! I had to consistently reinforce that our actions and purpose were around the patient. When the patient is at the center, decisions will always be made with the patient's best interest at heart. Although we had done well, this attitude would be the one that would help us sustain.

In this case, with my new awareness, it all lined up, and my team and I were able to do something to improve the safety for our patient. What I really learned was the true purpose of measuring and the purpose of our work.

For the project, I had several years' worth of data. I thought everyone would be really impressed with my ability to track and measure. Once I got into the project, I realized that I had numbers and goals, but I had no idea what caused those numbers. This project allowed me the time to focus on the causes. I learned not only how to get to the root and make the appropriate changes for improvement, but also that I was tracking and measuring a lot of things that may have no impact on the success of my department. After I completed the project, my team and I had a heart-to-heart. I really listened to them, and together we identified the critical few things that we needed to keep close tabs on. We didn't only track the numbers; when there was a dip, we looked at the situation to see what caused it. This took me back to the beginning of all of this. When we first started focusing on improvement, we never looked at the numbers; we looked at our behaviors. I did not look at impressing the CEO; I looked at impressing my dad.

Rhonda: Go Weight Watchers on your measures.

It is funny where life lessons come from. Once I joined Weight Watchers and lost a few pounds right away. They told me at my first meeting that it was very important to write down everything I ate. Well, I had definitely beaten the system. I did not write anything down, and I had still lost weight. In fact, I lost weight each week for the first three weeks. Then, on week four I approached the scale with all of the smugness of one who had outsmarted all of those program experts. Much to my disbelief, I had gained weight! This could not be correct. I had eaten what they had told me to. It must be the program, or perhaps there was a full moon throwing me off. All I knew was that it could not be because of my behavior. While the leader was conducting the meeting, I could not focus. Immediately afterward, I challenged her on how the program had failed me. Of course, she wanted to see my food diary. When I admitted I had not kept one, this all-knowing look crossed her face. She assumed that I had gained weight because I had not followed her silly rule.

Later that night, I could not stop thinking about this. I really focused and replayed everything I had eaten that day. I realized that because I had not written it down, I had eaten a larger portion and sometimes even the wrong foods. It was not all at once, but all of those little bites had added up. I realized with that program the food journal was simply a tool of accountability. My leader at work at the time was famous for saying, "What gets measured gets done." He said it every day, but he never practiced it. All of a sudden, I could connect the saying with the outcome. I had not measured my food intake, and therefore I did not do what I was supposed to do.

I have tried really hard since then to apply this knowledge to my work life as well. I really learned the truth of it during this transition. I saw departments implementing initiatives that were known best practices without measurement and therefore with temporary success. We are all tempted to only look at outcomes and not compliance. I had heard the story from many directors that they did not understand why their scores were dropping when they knew they were doing exactly what they were supposed to do. It took me back to the conversation with the Weight Watcher's counselor. I always asked if they had a measurement tool, and inevitably the answer was no. Over and over through the years, it was proven to me that without measurement, sustained outcomes were unlikely. One time, one of my friends who was an avid golfer gave me a great example to use. He said that any golfer worth his salt knows that if you want to improve your score, you do not look at the score, but you look at your swing. If you only measure the outcomes but never look at the actions that drive them, the outcomes will never change.

When talking with Greg one day, he was sharing his frustration that their scores had dropped. He had stopped measuring the compliance and was feeling the effects. The good news was that once he started measuring the compliance, his scores went back up immediately. Because he intervened before the new habits had been broken altogether, it was easier to recover than it was when the department had first started.

When I first became director of an operational department at this facility, it was a true test of my confidence. I knew the pressure to pull off success was great. I had been working with the other leadership and stressing the importance of all of the elements of success. If I failed in my own department, then I would look like a fraud. Strategic planning had never been as important to me as it was at this time. I carefully calculated how I would work accountability, recognition, skill development, and fun into the culture of the department. However, I knew that all of the efforts would be futile if not held together by measurement. Just like I had experienced pushback from the other leaders regarding measurement, I experienced it with my new direct reports as well. I actually had to let them fall a few times before they believed in the importance. Once it was proven to them, they became the biggest advocates of measuring actions. On any given day, I could ask them how they had achieved improvement, and they could tell me the exact detail that had led them to it. I believe that in order to achieve prolonged success one must know exactly what they did to get there. No matter the strategy, it is that knowledge that makes it happen. For example, we wanted to improve our compliance across the hospital with hand washing. The numbers went up, and the numbers went down. When we really started looking into it, we noticed that although there was no consistency for the hospital, there was some consistency for some departments. When we asked the departments whose scores fluctuated often what they were doing, they could not specifically say. When we asked the departments whose scores were consistent, rather than up or down, they knew exactly what they were or were not doing.

Through this realization, we were able to achieve hospital-wide success in a very short period of time in relation to hand washing. The first step was to put influencers into place. The influencers could not take the approach of "do it because I am saying so, and I am so smart." The influencers had to point out the deficit and simply offer a solution. The leadership had to back the influencers, though, just to give them the power they needed. So, the leadership set the expectations. "We expect you to wash your hands before you enter the room and when you leave the room—every time." Coaching opportunities had to be real time. If you see someone not wash their hands, the expectation was that you remind them. The coaches started out as designated individuals. The expectation was that we all coach, however. We gave the responsibility of secret observers, who recorded the compliance score, to the designated coaches and made everyone the opportunity coaches. My favorite story around this was when the CEO was going in to visit a patient and forgot to wash his hands. The unit secretary saw this happen and very politely reminded him. The compliance measurement was then shared, and noncompliance was not tolerated. When these steps were put into place, and everyone could tell you exactly what was driving the score, the scores soared above the goal and the stretch goal.

Purposeful measurement was holding all of our success together. Whenever we let the measurement slide or began measuring the wrong things, the outcomes diminished. You have to keep your eye on the ball—or risk getting hit!

The Lesson: What You Need to Know ...

Qaalfa: Get the organization interested in the outcome; get the employees interested in the precursors.
Kalina: Measures are means, not ends of.

Everyone wants to know about measures because they think the measures will let them know how they are doing in their transformation. To some degree, that is of course true. Global leaders were asked in a recent study what is the one question they want answered in relation to Customer Experience.[*] The largest number of global leaders (forty-three percent) said it was to know how to link Customer Experience to financial performance. In total, seventy-seven percent of global leaders of Customer Experience had a concern about the measurement of Customer Experience: whether to create a financial link to understand the drivers to help in a redesign or in terms of understanding the "full" Customer Experience.

Hospitals measure patient satisfaction like most organizations measure satisfaction. It's ubiquitous. These satisfaction scores are then sometimes used as a basis to determine bonuses and rewards for departments and individuals when their contribution aids meeting or exceeding targets. Satisfaction, however, is an output measure. It is dependent on the experience that customers (i.e., patients) receive. Knowing an output measure like satisfaction on its own tells you little about what needs to change to improve it. The scores describe your customers' attitudes, emotions, and behavior, which are essentially a result of the interaction they have with your organization. These tell you if you succeeded in achieving the goal, and they can be (and often are) treated as targets. They are also less actionable at the operational side because they indicate customers' response to your experience, rather than your direct experience performance. They give operational managers fewer clues about where to concentrate and what to do to effect change.

Nevertheless, outcome measures are important. They are tied to the organization's strategy. They represent what the organization wants to achieve. Hospitals in the United States now have the outcome measure of patient satisfaction directly tied to revenue via HCAHPS (Hospital Consumer Assessment of Healthcare Providers and Systems). Hospitals thus are directly incentivized to at least meet basic patient satisfaction levels.

---

[*] Steven Walden, *Global Beyond Philosophy*. 2011, Global Leaders Survey. http://www.beyond-philosophy.com/blog/2011-beyond-philosophy-global-customer-experience-management-survey

The HCAHPS survey not only asks patients how satisfied they are, but also asks several other questions regarding items that are thought to be precursors of satisfaction in hospitals. Examples of these HCAHPS precursor questions are as follows:

■ During this hospital stay, how often did nurses explain things in a way you could understand?
■ During this hospital stay, how often was the area around your room quiet at night?
■ Before giving you any new medicine, how often did hospital staff tell you what the medicine was for?

As you can see, these questions are about the experience itself, or to put it another way, these questions are focused on aspects of the experience that likely matter to patients directly. One of the interesting things about HCAHPS is that it was actually designed to help patients understand what should be important to them. The basic HCAHPS survey is set out such that there are several topic areas with a few precursor questions under each. The idea is that the organization can better understand what the underlying factors to the various outcome measures are. The HCAHPS structure creates a layered pyramid of understanding. At the top of the pyramid is patient satisfaction. The topic areas covered in the survey outline what some of the classic factors affecting patient satisfaction are: care from nurses, care from doctors, hospital physical environment, and so on.

Other industries may use the ACSI (American Customer Satisfaction Index) or other standard satisfaction survey instruments. They all will have questions that dig deeper than overall satisfaction and will give you clues regarding what underlying issues there might be that are preventing a higher overall satisfaction score. Similarly, most surveys looking at a Net Promoter Score® will do the same. The Net Promoter Score is based on asking customers the question: "How likely is it that you would recommend this experience to friends and family?" Customers answer on a zero- to ten-point scale; those who answer with nine or ten are called Promoters. Those who answer seven or eight are referred to as Passives. Those who answer from zero to six are Detractors. The Net Promoter Score is calculated as the percentage of customers who are Promoters minus the percentage of customers who are Detractors. HCAHPS also has its own similar question: "Would you recommend this hospital to your friends and family?"* However, in HCAHPS the answer selection is limited to four categorical choices: definitely no, probably no, probably yes, and definitely yes.

While outcome measures like Satisfaction and Recommendation are important strategically, precursor measures are important operationally. The precursor measures will give departmental managers and employees the information they need to begin to implement corrections. While the outcome measures are rallying

---

* HCAHPS survey questions. http://www.hcahpsonline.org/Files/HCAHPS%20V7%200%20 Appendix%20A1%20-%20HCAHPS%20Expanded%20Mail%20Survey%20Materials%20 (English)%20July%202012.pdf

points for the organization, the precursor measures play the key role in individual accountability and recognition. Precursor experience measures are actually indicators of the performance of the experience itself and relate to all the things that lead to the outcome. Rhonda refers to these as compliance measures. We like to call them precursor measures as compliance is often associated with legislation, safety, policies, and external rules. Precursor measures are attributes of the experience that are relevant to the final outcome success the organization is targeting.

Outcome measures are like the scale you use to weigh yourself; the precursor measures are akin to the diary that helps you keep track of what you eat. Both are important for success. Confusion, however, arises when outcome measures are treated as precursor measures and vice versa. Outcome measures are a reflection of how your customers respond to the experience you are trying to improve. Precursor measures indicate how elements of the experience that lead to the outcome are perceived by customers.

Think of measures as forming a kind of pyramid. At the top is an overall outcome measure you are interested in improving, like patient satisfaction. Even patient satisfaction is a precursor to, say, profitability. Underneath each measure will be other precursors that have an impact on the overall metric. Underneath those will be precursors to the precursors and so on. As you progress with your cultural transformation, the fullness of the measurement pyramid will become clearer and fuller for the organization. In other words, over time it will become clearer what impact (positive and negative) certain actions have on the outcome.

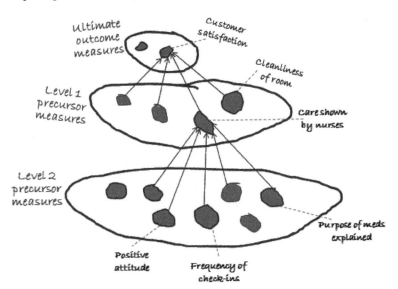

As Rhonda's golfer friend put it: "Any golfer worth his salt knows that if you want to improve your score, you do not look at the score, but you look at your swing." While the golf score may be the ultimate outcome, the directed action will have precursors of club selection, swing, and so forth. Each of these precursors will in turn have its precursors. Precursors to the swing might be the stance and grip plus many others. Likewise, "cleanliness of the room" may be one of the precursors to overall patient satisfaction. Cleanliness itself may be the outcome you are looking to improve and may have the precursor of a "well-stocked cleaning supply closet."

A goal of yours needs to be to identify the important precursor-outcome combinations as these will play a recurring role in your accountability and recognition investigations. Remember that recognition efforts kick in when specific behaviors have been identified and linked to a known success. The precursor measures can often serve the function of helping you to pinpoint where successful behaviors have occurred. Likewise, good precursor measures will also make your accountability efforts efficient. You may not always have the exact precursor measure that clearly identifies the root cause of a problem, but whichever ones you do have should help narrow down your investigation.

Here are the few things to know about measuring the experience:

1. Keep your eye on the ball. Regularly look at measures to identify precursor-outcome dyads to obtain a clearer picture of your own measures pyramid. Always seek to identify the reasons for your movement in scores so that employees have those at the top of their minds. These reasons should flow naturally from your accountability and recognition investigations. It is very likely that after some time you will identify recurring themes and topics that may need to be measured. Do not be afraid to include those and drop others. Measure attributes that are relevant to the outcome. The precursor measures are essentially attributes of the experience that directly drive or destroy your outcome measure of interest. You will need to identify the attributes (some call them touch points or factors) that have an impact on your customer experience and are directly responsible for the success of it. After his training course, Greg realized that the only relevant measure is the one that points out where the solution is: "I learned not only how to get to the root and make the appropriate changes for improvement, but also that I was tracking and measuring a lot of things that may have no impact on the success of my department." There are many ways to identify the key attributes of the experience. Greg talked to his staff at the Daily Huddles and kept track of the important attributes: "Together we identified the critical few things that we needed to keep close tabs on. We didn't only track the numbers; when there was a dip, we looked at the situation to see what caused it." Rhonda found examples in best performers: "When we asked the departments whose scores fluctuated often what they were doing, they could not specifically say. When we asked the departments whose scores were consistent, rather than up or down, they knew exactly what they were or were not doing."

2. As important as measures are, do not overburden yourself with them. They are just tools to help you do the right thing; they are not the totem to be adored. Treat them like a starting point of your accountability and recognition investigations, not an end result. After the failure he experienced, Greg went into overdrive to measure everything, assuming it was the best way to gain control over the situation: "I tracked everything and prided myself that we had more than twenty goals for our team. All of this measuring took a lot of energy and time. I was robbing my team of the energy needed to make improvements and to grow and develop." This is exhausting and unnecessary. You will of course go down some blind measurement alleys on occasion, but you should always attempt to refine and locate the relevant precursor-outcome relationships. Your measures should all fit in your measurement pyramid and form some precursor-outcome dyad.

3. Measure your customers' perception and the emotional experience; physical reality and experience are not the same. What you do is only as good as how it is perceived. Many call centers measure waiting times on the phone because they know customers hate waiting, and it is the reason for decreased satisfaction scores. But, even a minute may be too long a wait when the line is silent, and 5 minutes may be perceived as 5 seconds when entertaining jokes are being played during waiting time. Perception can be altered by subtle clues and emotional levers. Emotional levers are little additions to the experience that are aimed at creating a positive emotional experience for customers. For example, a smile on the face may not be relevant to how good a job the doctor does in absolute technical terms, but it can have a huge impact on how confident and comfortable the patient feels and therefore how satisfied the patient is with the overall experience. It is a matter of addressing the emotional needs of customers. In 2005, when Qaalfa and Rhonda were investigating the experience other hospitals in the system gave their cancer patients, they found that patients expected at least thirty percent of the experience to be aimed at addressing emotional well-being. Many hospitals (or businesses) know that emotions matter, but not many of them purposefully measure and track them.

4. Attach coaching to measurement. Measures are the starting point of your accountability and recognition investigations and discussions. In your team conversations and feedback sessions, your measures should allow you to better connect with individual actions and behaviors. Measures are generally a waste of time and money if they do not help you understand and act on some precursor-outcome situation. Coaching is important as a follow-up to the accountability and recognition investigations. In accountability, you will of course coach the employee on alternative behaviors that should lead to better measures in the future. Of course, if you have been doing recognition

investigations as recommended, you will be in a position to spread that best practice when you are doing your coaching. Once you have identified the reasons for success or failure, spread the learning and turn it (i.e., the learning) into practices. As with recognition and appreciation, this is best done when done informally. Rhonda stated this clearly: "Coaching opportunities had to be real time. If you see someone not wash their hands, the expectation was that you remind them. The coaches started out as designated individuals. The expectation was that we all coach, however." As with the other principles, managers will most likely start first; peer influencers will start following as they become more engaged, and it will spread gradually across teams until everyone in the organization feels empowered to coach and feels entitled to correct colleagues when they see misconduct. The confidence to do this will be enhanced when peers understand the precursor-outcome measure connection. This understanding will grow as you and other influencers coach based on accountability and recognition of investigation evidence. As with most everything we have said so far, the measure-coach principle applies to the whole organization. Remember: Rhonda's "favorite story around this was when the CEO was going in to visit a patient and forgot to wash his hands. The unit secretary saw this happen and very politely reminded him." Make no exceptions.

It is not by chance that the measurement chapter is toward the end of the book. If you impose measures and ask employees to police colleagues without having created engagement or without practicing recognition, you will only build stress and frustration. Without the work of Engagement Bowtie activity, measures will most likely be tools used to deflate morale. Another clue regarding whether you are effective in bowtie activities will be if you are getting less reaction, like "It's not us," "We don't know," "Wasn't me," or just passive silence. When there is engagement, interest in and use of the measures will seem easy and natural. You will not see many rolling eyes or hear sighs, and you will see accountability, recognition, and proactive attitude in solving issues. Measures will be just a tool used to better identify and structure discussions and actions.

Chapter 9

Action Program Spirit to Achieve Excellence

Greg: People will be interested in your story.

Rhonda came rushing into my office one day, very excited. This was one of the times that always made me chuckle a little. We had formed such a partnership that we worked seamlessly together. We were quite opposites by nature, though. She bubbled over when I soaked it in. She announced that our hospital had won a national award for our success, and that as a result we were invited to speak at a national conference and tell our story. I was as nervous as she was excited. I had never spoken in front of a large group and quite frankly found the idea intimidating. She waved away my fears as nonsense and assured me there was nothing to be afraid of. I remained unconvinced. I was flattered at being asked to share our story, but I had no desire to do it. I decided she could tell the story, and I would be in the audience. She insisted that it had to be a joint effort. Rhonda is one of those people who do not need a lot of time to think about things. I, however, do. I made an excuse about having to get to a meeting so she would leave my office. Once she had left, the fear really took over. Just thinking about it convinced me it was not going to happen. Even later that night, I felt a little queasy at the thought. I was definitely going to tell Rhonda I was not going to do it.

Rhonda: Shout your success from the rooftop; it's part of the process, too.

I could not believe it! I had sent in the submission never believing we would actually win the award. This award was presented to very few hospitals across the country. You had to show proof of outcomes across the board—and we had done it! This hospital that had struggled with so many challenges had done it! Sometimes it seemed that we were pushed back two steps for every step we moved forward. It sometimes felt like luck did not seem to go our way. Through sheer determination and will, we had arrived. All along, I believed that the success was enough without recognition for it. How silly of me. Had I not stood up to several of my peers and stressed the importance of recognition? Why did I feel the need to have some false sense of humility and pretend recognition was not important to me? Well, now that our hospital was getting recognition on the national level, I realized how much impact it has on you. I wanted to shout it from the rooftop.

My first stop was Greg's office. I could not wait to tell him that we won and had been invited to present our story at a national conference. I was so excited as I told him that there would probably be three or four hundred people there just wanting to hear about our journey. Wow! He completely missed the point, though. He was actually scared to present in front of the crowd. He was even willing to pass up the opportunity and let me present alone. Was he crazy? This was the chance of a lifetime. How many times would you get to enjoy this kind of success, let alone be asked to tell the story to an audience like this? Then, our conversation was cut short because he had to go to a meeting. I kind of felt like maybe the meeting was just an excuse to get rid of me.

Next, I burst straight into the CEO's [chief executive officer's] office. I could not wait to tell him that we were being publicly recognized for all of the blood, sweat, and tears we had shed to make these improvements. It was like showing your father your invitation to the National Honor Society. He was so proud of our achievement. It was that look on his face and the words he shared that made all of this worth it. Even more than the trophy and opportunity to speak, I was overwhelmed by his admiration.

Greg and I had already planned to meet to discuss what we would present. I had already begun working on the slide deck for the presentation. I was a little overwhelmed by emotion when I thought about how much I had learned from Greg and how much I owed him for this success. I could never have made all of these ideas work without him, the executive group, my peers, and all of the front line. I thought about the first day I walked in and how unwelcome I had felt. When I was little, I dreamed of changing the world. My dad said to me one day: "If you want to make that happen, you are going to have to be the persistence against the resistance." Now, all of that seemed like it was in the far distance.

Greg: Be prepared to take some credit.

The next day as I drove in to work, I practiced what I was going to say to Rhonda to get out of doing this presentation. I was going to explain to her that she deserved the credit and so should be the one to present. Besides, it was really all of her ideas we had adopted.

I walked in to Rhonda's office, and she was already working on the slides to present. I was beginning to lose all of the courage I had mustered up on the drive over. I was almost as afraid to tell her I was not going to co-present as I was to present in the first place. I was just going to sit beside her and help her with the slides and then break it to her. After all, I should at least help with the slides since I planned to abandon her at the podium.

Rhonda: One does not simply implement initiatives.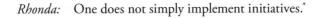*

I wanted to hold nothing back in our presentation. If this audience was going to invest ninety minutes in listening to us, I wanted to give them their time's worth. I also wanted to see hospitals across the country improve the Patient Experience. The main idea that I wanted to stress was that that implementing initiatives would not lead to success. You can do any one of a thousand initiatives and not achieve success. The important thing was in creating the culture in which the team can thrive and the initiatives can work.

In reaffirmation of my belief that you have to know the specific behaviors that drove the success—and the behaviors that lead to failure—it was very rewarding to realize that Greg and I knew just that. It gave me the confidence to know that this success would stick. The presentation seemed to fly from our fingertips onto the slides. It really took very little thought at all. We had been operating in such a way that our actions were like reflexes—reflexes honed by doing all of things mentioned in this book.

At the conference, we would share how to build a culture. We knew the audience would want to know about the tools and activities that we used to accomplish this because that is how most strategic thinkers categorize things. We began listing the tools on the slides. These fit into three categories. The categories included communication and motivation, skill development, and fun and recognition.

We started with sharing the tools and activities around communication and motivation. We practiced a huddle every day in each department. On a weekly basis, we published some talking points about what was going on around the hospital and some basic expectations. When each leader began using these five

---

* This is a common meme originating from the *Lord of the Rings* movie series.

minutes to talk with their team about their struggles and successes, it became a much cherished time of each shift. It was not to just talk, though. The practice was to share ideas and solutions as a team, not to whine together.

The huddles were reinforced by the department and hospital leadership rounding on employees. The roundings helped the leadership to really know what was going on in the building and to get a true picture of the culture. The leadership team rounded on the staff and patients in the departments they supported. It sounds really simple. We have learned that everyone says they round. In fact, there are hours spent walking around and waving at employees that result in no outcome. The real magic in rounding does not occur during the first or even second conversation you have with someone. The third time, or so, when the barrier is let down you get the real story. The people begin to trust you. The first time they share something with you and you really listen and react is when you have created an influencer. As soon as they tell someone about your investment in them, they are working as an agent to change the culture, even if they are not aware of it. It also cannot be assumed that everyone will get "how to" round. We had to implement the rounding but then follow that with observing and coaching the rounders.

Leaders attend many meetings. In fact, we attend so many meetings that we begin to avoid them like the plague. I would almost bet that many of you actually got a little bit of a negative feeling when you saw the word meeting on this page. Remember though that an engaged workforce needs to feel included and informed. Some leaders, however, are not natural-born communicators. We began putting the monthly communication points in a format and sending it out to the leaders to use at their team meetings. Not all leaders used it equally, but all used it effectively. Just like we had measured hand-washing compliance and effectiveness with observers, we measured meeting compliance and effectiveness by observing. When we realized someone needed coaching in this area, we did it. Remember, expectations must be set, and noncompliance cannot be tolerated. It is central to accountability.

To reinforce this communication, our CEO held quarterly town hall sessions. These were never mandatory, and at first they were so scarcely attended you could "see the tumbleweeds" moving through the room. Even if there were only one or two in attendance, however, he gave the same investment as if there was standing room only; after all, those employees in attendance had invested their time in listening to him. He engaged those employees through those efforts, and thus more influencers were made.

The next category was skill development. We had much success around motivation through our communication efforts. We had many people out there willing to create the change, but we had to make sure they were skilled to do it. The very first thing we realized was that our frontline staff did not know the basic expectations. We decided to have education courses taught by the chiefs. Each chief would conduct eleven 1-hour sessions in a month. Those sessions went into the purpose and values of our system and the behaviors expected. They were classroom lectures, and since they were mandatory, they were well attended. I cannot say everyone reported to those sessions with the desire to align with the values of the company. I can say, though, that many of them were reached in those sessions, and the commitment for many was made. We learned it was not always about teaching; often, it was about reaching the audience. That first session led us to the realization that we expected an outcome of a certain patient experience, but not even all of the leadership could explain what it looked like or how to get there. So, we realized we needed to have another course the next quarter. This one led to another course and then another. These quarterly education sessions became a reliable tool to maintain our culture. Soon, the courses became more like workshops. Eventually, the workshops evolved into skills labs.

In the skills labs, we put the employee in their own work environment. Nurses, lab techs, and environmental service workers were placed in patient rooms; imaging technicians were in an x-ray room; and so on. We placed them in real-life situations and had them role-play scenarios that we got from the patient comments. We were able to assess when they needed in-depth coaching. We found that many of them felt a new level of comfort to ask for help with challenging situations. The lines of communication were opened up, and a more trusting environment was created. This was followed by more real-time observing and coaching.

The frontline staff needed to develop their skills, but the leadership team was asking for development as well. Each quarter, we had an all-day development work-shop. The agenda was set by the participants. If someone was particularly good at a skill that their peers needed help with, they ran the lab for that skill. All of the leaders were there to learn and share. Not only did our knowledge and abilities flourish through those days, but also our relationships were improved.

We knew that the leaders could not be everywhere all of the time, and that not all staff would feel comfortable with peer coaching. We asked for a group of employees to apply for a newly created role. The role was that of a coach to work in their normal department. There was no additional financial compensation, and they were still expected to do their jobs. I wondered if anyone would even want to do this! To my surprise, however, there was no shortage of people applying. After an interview with the CEO, the service excellence advisors were chosen. They then participated in a biweekly training session to develop their coaching skills.

The final category was around fun and recognition. Just as real-time opportunities are important for coaching behavior change, they are vital for encouraging the desired behavior. We utilized cafeteria coupons and gift shop tokens that people could use for instant awards when they witnessed a coworker or direct report doing well. We wanted those stories to spread throughout the building. Our goal was continuous reinforcement for all to see. We began sending the stories out through e-mails and posting cards that employees used to recognize one another. These were created when a patient or physician recognized an employee as well. The first month we used those cards, we had less than fifty cards. The CEO challenged me that he wanted at least 400 per month. Before long, we had doubled his goal.

As the stories circulated, a culture was emerging where people wanted to do things to be recognized for. We began a monthly celebration, called the iWOWed [I Work on Wonderful Every Day] event for those that were consistently recognized. It was a tiered program where people received gifts according to the number of times they were recognized. The first award was a shirt that could be worn on Fridays. The blue shirt was unique to these recipients and could not be bought. Soon, we had a sea of blue shirts every Friday. This celebration evolved over the years. It became the place to celebrate all accomplishments. In these monthly celebration events, we celebrated departmental awards, hospital awards, and even introduced major equipment purchases that were designed to make the work easier. The staff looked forward to those celebrations. We began having them at lunchtime and serving a meal so more people could attend. Eventually, we took the celebration to the departments every other month. We did this at five in the morning and again in the afternoon to reach more of the staff. The rule we stood by was if we did something during the day, we repeated it at night. Our night shift team felt very included and therefore was more engaged in the culture.

In addition to the iWOWed celebration, events were planned to have fun as well. Once a month, we had celebration days where we took a cart of snacks around. We called this Thankful Thursday. The idea was that we let the employees know we appreciated them, but we asked if they had anyone they wanted to recognize as well. Once, the Joint Commission dropped in on one of these days. We questioned whether or not we should continue with the plan for that month. We took the chance and did it. The surveyors thought it was a great idea. We also had Hospital Olympics during Hospital Week; everyone became very competitive during those games! The roped-off portion of the parking lot filled with teams from each department. There was always a variety of uniforms and team names. The players often switched out so that more people from each department could participate in the fun. The games included urinal bowling, bedpan catch, room cleaning and tray-making relays, personal protective equipment jump rope races, hula-hooping around our successes, and many other events the teams vied to finish in—all of this practicing and laughing in an effort to take home the gold. In this case, the gold was a bedpan and urinal spray-painted gold and filled with candy.

We finished the slides with a few graphs of our results. As I reviewed the slides once more, I felt very satisfied with the actions and the results.

Greg: The story belongs to all of us.

It took us a few hours to put our thoughts onto these slides. As I began to watch our story unfold into a slide show format, all of my fears began to go away. I realized I knew this. I knew exactly what we had done to get the award. Once I realized it was just our story I was telling, not Rhonda's story, but our entire team's story, I was no longer afraid to tell it. I was still a little intimidated by the number of people that would be watching, but the thought of being able to touch that many healthcare leaders and therefore that many patients across the country inspired me to want to tell it to as large an audience as possible. More than twenty years ago, I had promised my dad that I wanted to make it easier for patients to get care. I finally realized what that meant. I was supposed to work at a community hospital and make it easier for those patients to get care. I was also supposed to present in front of that crowd because someone needed to hear our message. Our patients were definitely benefitting from our success, and there were patients all over that could benefit as well. So, it was determined: We would go to the conference, accept the award, and tell our story—together.

Rhonda: Success is not in your future if all you are interested in is a few initiatives.

I looked over at the crowd waiting to hear us speak. I looked over at Greg who smiled in return. I looked at my colleagues in the audience who were there to cheer us on. I gave a silent nod to my grandmother and began our story.

When we were done, we received a number of questions. Many of these questions were about what we did, the initiatives. One of the main messages Greg and I wanted to leave behind was that the success came from the behaviors we and others displayed as we implemented those initiatives. Although we stressed this in the presentation, we quickly realized that what many people tended to hear was this initiative or that initiative. The questions tended to be something like how did you structure your skills lab and so on. These kinds of questions would allow one to take an idea and run with it, which is great—except that we also got the feeling that many people were more concerned with implementing the initiative than making it successful. Also, remember the example of people following an initiative because they are told to, which does not always lead to engagement. To completely work this into your very foundation, the employees must think with the patient in the center of the decisions.

In subsequent presentations, Greg and I refined the message, boiling it down to engagement coaching, measurement, accountability, and recognition. We were getting closer to being able to deliver the message in a way that would be heard correctly by the majority of the audience. We approached Qaalfa and Kalina to help further refine the message because we wanted to spell out the principles even more clearly. The four of us have had many discussions and given several presentations in the United States and Europe. We can tell that the message is getting through to more people, but we also recognize that many others approach a Patient Experience cultural transformation as a project and are simply looking for a few killer activities to implement. We needed to more fully explain the true source of our success. Thus, the idea of this book was formed.

Kalina: Don't fail to see the forest because of the trees.

The first time I heard Rhonda and Qaalfa tell this story, I could immediately see the relevance of their learning to other industries: telecoms, financial services, pharmaceuticals, retail, and so on. The truth is, the principles described in this book cut across sectors and markets because they describe the path to cultural change, whatever that new culture is. Organizations often say "My business is different." The funny thing is, whenever I describe the story but use customer instead of patient, they all become enthralled.

Rhonda is one of the best storytellers I have listened to, and she uses that talent to great effect. Other industries that have listened to her tell her story have been as enlightened as I was when I first heard it. Hopefully, the influencers and true leaders out there will recognize the value of it.

The Lesson: What You Need to Know …

Qaalfa: Be true to the intent; otherwise, it's just busy work.
Kalina: Initiatives have an expiry date; mindset does not.

Achieving Customer Experience excellence is a matter of cultural transformation. Initiatives by themselves have an expiry date on their effectiveness: As a one-off, they are only effective as long as the situation in which they were implemented remains unchanged, which is never the case. Think of all the potential a new information technology system generally brings. Now, think of all the ways it does not deliver. We do not have to specify the system because this scenario is so common that it is the norm. One of the reasons for this disparity is because not enough effort was put into making sure employees would adhere and use the system the way it was described when it was sold and installed. It is a cultural problem. Systems usually can do all the things indicated. The problem is not a technological one; it is a people one. People have not made the switch to see the benefit of doing whatever extra or different steps are required to make full use of the system. What is required to get the return on investment from that system is a mindset change on the part of the employees who must use that system.

A cultural mind shift will create and ensure successful implementation of initiatives on a perpetual basis. Rhonda made a firm statement: "You can do any one of a thousand initiatives and not achieve success. The important thing was in creating the culture in which the team can thrive and the initiatives can work." In other words, the spirit of the law is more important than the letter of law in customer experience. The spirit of the law allows us to address both the rational and the emotional needs of employees who we are asking to change. The letter of the law of customer experience appeals most to the rational side of things.

The ultimate goal of a cultural transformation is to create influencers. The influencers are essentially engaged staff who spread the enthusiasm and knowledge like fire. They are alert, focused, and most important, genuinely interested in bettering the experience they deliver through the work they do. The initiatives will be successful because of the efforts of influencers. Initiatives carried out by unengaged employees are essentially tick-box exercises and will only be successful while their implementation is heavily policed. The success that stems from such policing tends to dissipate as soon as the policing ceases. We referred to this as a kind of Hawthorne effect in Chapter 4, "Connect to Engage."

Rhonda and Greg deployed a number of initiatives at Community General. Some of these became standard practices there, but none of these would have worked had there not been true understanding of the spirit of the law. These practices are just a way of manifesting the spirit of the law.

- Daily Huddles: fifteen-minute meetings to discuss Patient Experience expectations and progress
- Rounding: walks around the floor to visit patients and spot customer experience-aligned or -misaligned behaviors
- Monthly team meetings: with a standardized meeting agenda that emphasizes the importance of Patient Experience and expectations around it
- Quarterly skills labs: workshops and sessions delivered by staff for staff with the intent of sharing Patient Experience knowledge
- Service excellence advisors: employees who will observe and informally coach colleagues on excellence in customer experience
- Instant awards: coupons, iWoW, thank you cards to show appreciation and recognition of employees' work
- Monthly celebrations (blue shirt Friday): tiered program by which people receive gifts according to the number of times they were recognized for successful Patient Experience delivery
- Once-a-month Fun Day: a day to enjoy and relax with employees
- Precursor metrics: specific experience-related activities that are the root causes of success or failure

We have seen companies use these or similar initiatives but fail to achieve success when applied without the appropriate spirit and intent. The intent of an activity is more difficult to put in writing, but here are a few pointers regarding how your activity should look and feel:

- Serve to lead
  - If you are new to your role, early on demonstrate that you care about the employees. Look through employee suggestions or simply pay attention to

water cooler talk. Determine a change that would be widely noticed and one that you think people will talk about informally. Make the change and make sure it is known by a few who are responsible for the change; this is not to be done via e-mail announcement, flyers, or posters. You will simply want a few of the respected employees to know. You will be relying on them to spread the word on their own accord. So, it is important to choose the change appropriately. It is important that this does not appear to be a gimmick on your part. You must believe the change is necessary or else it may come across as a ploy.

- Prepare to respond to employees' sacrifice in times of crises. Your organization probably has a contingency plan to cover process and systems. You should have a crisis response plan to appreciate employees who actually sacrifice to keep things going. At Community General, the CEO took the extraordinary steps of ordering hard-to-get fuel and water for employees who saw the hospital through during a hurricane. Your emergency need not be so drastic. It could be a public relations disaster or even coverage for an employee who is sick for an extended period of time. The care and appreciation you show for an employee who steps up his or her game in response to a crisis will not go unnoticed. To be clear, the appreciation that works best is one that shows care and thinking through that employee's sacrifice and situation. If your appreciation is relatively small, be prepared for a little cynicism at first. It may take a few repeated efforts for your genuineness to sink in. Regardless of what the appreciation is, deliver it with sincerity and cut the formalities.

■ Personalize to motivate
- Obtain an understanding of which employees are influential with their peers. This is less about formal authority and more about who employees trust. Put that list together in your head. You will want to try to reach these individuals first.
- Talk to employees at all levels. The point of these chats will be to see why employees are working in the hospital or what the hospital means to them in their lives. These conversations do not happen according to a schedule. So, these are not interviews; you are looking for what this person is passionate about and how the hospital fits in with that. You do not want employees to think that you are interviewing them, so these conversations are natural and of normal length. You may not have permission to probe too deeply at first, so you will have to think of this as happening over time for some employees. You will not be able to have these conversations with all employees. If you can, target employees who are influential with their peers. The idea is that these employees will naturally speak about this interest as yours, and when you are successful, they will shift to describing it as their own. You will have touched something in them.

They will each explain it in a personal manner, but the idea is that you will help rekindle that flame of motivation within them.

- Help employees see the experience as your customers do; give them the time and opportunity for it. The purpose is to remind them of the importance the experience they help deliver has in customers' lives. This is especially obvious in healthcare as the experience healthcare workers provide patients with is so immediately impactful. The intrinsic satisfaction of helping others is a huge magnet for attracting people to the industry.

- For others who are more distant and resistant—the naysayers—you may have to show a bit of "stick" (i.e., formal authority). First, you need to make sure you have some stick to use. Bluntly speaking, if you are in a position to hurt someone's career (promotion, bonus, tenure), then you have stick. You may not have it directly. If you have to go through others, you will want to shore this relationship up pronto. Get that person onboard and understanding that you will need their support in possibly drastic ways early on when the Patient Experience program is in its infancy. The Patient Experience program will not be the only thing going on at the hospital, so it is important that employees pay attention. You will be able to reach a few employees more or less immediately. Others will require a push. Even Greg needed a push from the CEO. Rhonda was there to show him the way. The CEO literally told one experienced nurse to leave when she said she would not change (see Chapter 4, "Connect to Engage").

- You probably will only have to use the stick early on to show how serious the organization is. Word will spread quickly. If you are generous with using your carrots, the cultural change will begin. If you are not generous with your carrots, frustration and anger will take hold, and the most you will achieve is compliance, but only under heavy policing.

■ Connect to engage
- Create a list of the job clusters in your organization. This could be as simple as a list of the departments. If you are in a large organization, this list could be long. Then, for each job cluster, create at least two levels, manager and employee. You may be able to be more specific for some departments from the beginning. You should be able to be more specific for all job clusters in time.

- Within each category, you will want to craft/collect stories that show how that job cluster has an impact on the Customer Experience in a profound way. Rhonda told the story of how she was able to connect with the housekeeper about how important his role was in making her grandmother's experience. You will want to have stories at the ready to tell at the drop of a hat. You will probably be telling these stories at unexpected unplanned times, so you will want to be ready. It will probably be easy for you to do this for the customer-facing roles. It will be harder as you go further behind the scenes into the back office. You need not complete the entire table shown in this chapter in one go, but you should have it as your goal to be able to tell a story for each category in time. You may use the same story several times—you will just want to tell it from the angle relevant to that job cluster. This is similar to the famous approach NASA took in getting all of their employees, no matter their role, to understand their job was to get a man on the moon.

- Although you may do this as a mental exercise, we recommend actually writing it down. This will allow you to see where you have gaps and keep tabs of new stories you collect as you go along. Your list may look something like this:

	Department 1	Department 2	Department 3
manager	Story 1 suited to managers of department 1	Story 1 suited to managers of department 2	Story 2 suited to managers of department 3
staff	Story 1 suited to staff of department 1	Story 2 suited to staff of department 2	Story 3 suited to staff of department 3

- As soon as you have a few of these determined, look for opportunities to tell these stories. You may want to read up on storytelling if you have lost the art of it. It is good practice to end with a connection to something that is going on right now. So, if you were telling Rhonda's story, you might want to end it with "so with all the things that are not going her way right now, you could very well be making all the difference in the world to Mrs. Johnson in room 214." You will want to incorporate these stories into everything you are doing: attending management meetings, seeing an employee performing in a lackluster manner in the hall, having water cooler chats, and so on. Your tone should be the same as you would use in a regular conversation. The more formal you sound, the more it will sound like someone else's story, issue, and concern.
- Express appreciation for employees doing things in a manner consistent with your Patient Experience ethos. This is most effective when done informally and when it feels spontaneous to the employees. As much as possible, begin co-opting other senior managers or influential employees to do the same. You may have to provide light training on how to show

appreciation. Often, a thank you or a pat on the back for a specifically named act is all that it takes.

- It is great if these co-opted leaders and influencers show appreciation in opportune times in the middle of doing other things. For example, it is effective if a senior executive says thank you to an accountant for creating the new report that will make it easier to identify patients who may need a bit more financial counseling on their complex billing. How will the senior executive know who and what to thank? That is your job. You will feed your co-opted thankers with the names and stories. These people then, whenever the opportunity arises, can show their appreciation. You will know you are on the right track when your co-opted thankers begin to ask you for a few more names of people to thank. You will not want to overload your thankers with an endless list of names and stories. Do not necessarily expect them to study and memorize the list. What you want is for them to actually begin to show the appreciation and for that word to spread among employees that something is changing: People are starting to say thank you.

■ Fail, then account
  - Make clear responsibilities (push accountability) and make note of those employees who take on responsibility (pull accountability). You will start with your direct reports and with your colleagues at the senior level. Again, having a bit of "stick insurance" always helps in the early stages when talking to your own peers or those who may be in higher positions than you.
  - Spot failure. Use a different term if you want to soften it. You will have to get those around you able to spot it and publicly accept that the behavior or practice is or was a failure. If this simple step is not taken, it will be difficult to correct the behavior. Often, the precursor measures will help in this light. Not all behavior is measured, however. While out in the organization, your eyes and ears will have to become attuned to spotting breakdowns in behavior and practices.
  - If the issue is simple, you may immediately engage in some discreet, on-the-spot coaching. Refer to Rhonda's "red/blue card" idea mentioned in Chapter 5, "Fail, then Account." It is a great way of allowing employees to signal each other nonverbally, from a distance, and immediately. This allows for coaching to occur anytime, anywhere in a nonthreatening manner.
  - When failure is more team/department based, you will want to have a thorough review based on all available information. It works best if you have been communicating performance consistently throughout. The objective of the drains up should be on correction and solution. To apply the right correction or solution, you will need to investigate the root cause.

Be careful and cognizant of employees who have not yet displayed pull accountability thinking that the investigation is about playing the blame game. This can be tricky at first, but if you keep your ultimate focus on the correction/solution you can reduce or even prevent this blame game culture from taking hold. Make sure you have a failure at the baseline so that you can celebrate when the behavior has been overturned.

■ Succeed, then recognize
  - You will most likely already have some sort of formal recognition program. That is great, but do give it an honest assessment. If that program is not valued by employees, you will have to make the assessment regarding whether the program can be salvaged or whether it is better to start your own recognition program.
  - Build a program that allows for broad recognition if you can. Programs that single out one or two exceptional people tend to focus on the extraordinary efforts that they have taken given a particular situation. Since most employees will not be presented with those situations, they would not be in a position to be recognized. Rhonda's blue shirt program is an example of a broad-based program. It allows all employees to aspire to join that club.
  - Like with accountability, you may have spotted little behaviors that you want to appreciate by showing that employee a blue card. If you can begin to get employees to blue card good behaviors and then send you a text or e-mail about a particular one, you may build the burgeoning foundation of an employee-led recognition program that is respected by employees.
  - It may sometimes be necessary for you to investigate successes to determine what the precursors to that success were. In this way, you will be in a better position to talk and spread best practice—and spot the antithesis of that best practice. You hold a meeting to discuss the success and what caused it. Most employees are not used to having a meeting to discuss the background of a success. That meeting will be rewarding for employees concerned, especially if they understand that you will be using theirs as an example of best practice for other departments.

■ Inject fun to energize
  - Creativity is the name of the game here. It matters not at all if you prefer to call it innovation or creativity. The idea is to add contrast to your program. It will help break up the monotony of everyday work. You would do well to have a couple of books on workshops and team-building exercises as these might give you a few ideas. If your organization's culture is very strong and staid, start off small, such as meeting outside instead of inside. Greg started with having team meetings at a park. If you brainstorm with a group for suggestions early on, consider even the most sarcastic remarks as fodder for a potential idea. Rhonda turned a

snide remark about taking the team on a cruise into a weeklong office cruise idea.

■ Measure to coach
  – Begin to create a measurement pyramid. Identify the main strategic measures you are looking to impact. These may be bottom line (e.g., revenue) or next in line (e.g., customer satisfaction or recommendation).
  – Then, think through the precursor experience measure that affects that outcome measure you just listed. If you have developed a long list of precursors, narrow that list using the following criteria:
    • Can you get consistent measures for it?
    • Can you have an impact on it? If the answer is an honest "no," drop it. If the real answer is "partially," then you may want to see if there is another level of precursor for that particular metric.
    • Is it closely related to other measures? If so, you may be able to use one of these closely related measures.
  – This will be your hypothesis measurement pyramid. You can refine this by talking to your colleagues. These conversations will be helpful because they will help the organization understand and accept the notion of the relationships. This will of course come into play with your push accountability hat on.
  – Be familiar with measures that others are using. Understand if the measures have helped determine what led to a failure or success in an accountability or recognition investigation.
■ Collect information from customers on the relevant measures. This not only may be in formal surveys but also look to obtain a feel for things simply by asking patients questions related to the measures in your pyramid. This informal feedback may provide the earliest signs that things or working well or not.

Central to the title of this book is the notion of a successful Patient Experience implementation. That is only possible via a cultural transformation. For most organizations, the cultural transformation will require a change in mindset. We cannot emphasize enough the point that this will only happen by following the spirit of the actions outlined in this book. Your activities may be designed differently. They may be more technologically savvy or less so. They may go by different names. Your awards may cost more. You may be working with a large team, or you may be a department of one. If you apply the spirit of what is included here, you will move the organization; in the worst case, you will discover that senior management is only paying lip service to the notion of Patient Experience improvement. However, with HCAHPS (Hospital Consumer Assessment of Healthcare Providers and Systems) very much a reality for U.S. hospitals, you have some weight behind your words. Use it.

Chapter 10

Get Help to Be Independent

Rhonda: Fish: to give is OK; to teach how is forever.

On the plane to London, I was thinking about the last three years. The harder you work for something, the more you appreciate it. I had enjoyed success throughout my career, and I feel I had worked hard. I learned so many lessons from this hospital. I often find it amusing that I thought I was coming here to teach them a thing or two, but they taught me multitudes of things. I learned there is a huge difference between working hard and challenging work. My first day at this hospital, one of my peers asked me what made me qualified to work here. I did not pay her much mind at the time, but I really started to think about the answers to that question.

In the years prior to coming to Community General, I had the opportunity to work with a consulting group. Any time I had worked with consultants before, it was not such a good experience. I thought consultants were people who came in and told you what to do and "got out of Dodge" before they could be blamed for the lack of sustained results. The last group of consultants I worked with was different, or maybe it was me who was different. I think before I was just looking for the silver bullet. For example, if consultants come in because you need help with cost containment, they can tell you where to cut costs. There are immediate results because you followed their actions. However, after they leave, if your behavior does not change, the results do not last. It is like that old proverb: "If you give a man a fish you feed him for a day. If you teach a man to fish you feed him for a lifetime."

In 2004, I heard Colin Shaw of Beyond Philosophy present a talk at a conference and arranged to speak to him about what we were doing at the hospital system. His group had interesting things to say, but like my experience with all consultants, I really did not expect much in practice. However, the hospital system had reached a plateau and needed to find a way to progress. We had been implementing Six Sigma, but I knew that that was not going to improve our patients' experience in the way we wanted. These consultants had a track record in other industries, and that gave us the confidence to give them a shot. This is when I met Qaalfa, who led the project.

Qaalfa was smooth. He explained a number of solutions that they were going to put in place. He explained everything clearly, but I now recognize that he was not talking about initiatives, although that is what I was hearing at the time; he was really establishing a foundation for our cultural transformation.

Qaalfa and his colleagues did not just do their work; they made me do it too. It was not about implementing initiatives like rounding, it was about seeing things differently. After working with Qaalfa, I really understood what it meant and how to see things from a patient's point of view. It is just now, on this plane, that I am realizing that I always thought we were given initiatives, and we just made those initiatives work. As I think about it, many of the original initiatives that we implemented are no longer in place, not because they were bad, but because life and business is ever evolving. I am seeing the real beauty of working with Qaalfa and his colleagues. They did not make me dependent on their initiatives but taught me how to see things differently and evolve with the inevitable change.

Another lesson learned is that it is not a weakness to have to ask for help. The weakness can come if you utilize that help as a crutch and not as development. In my past role, we had made much improvement in creating our experience for our patients, but we had reached a plateau. We had to take a chance on bringing in outside help. We considered it an investment, not an expense. When you hire a personal trainer to help you get in shape, you have results because the trainer is behind you, emotionally supporting and pushing you. If you learn the technique and self-motivation, that investment can stay with you forever. It is the same thing in business with consultants. By working with Qaalfa, I gained knowledge that I have used over and over. In fact, it was really seamless how I applied that knowledge in my new position at Community General. I was hungry and had been taught how, so I just started to fish.

Qaalfa: Spot the need rather than the want.

In that first meeting with Rhonda and others, it was evident that they needed some help establishing a foundation for change. They had bold plans and even higher ambition. Their driver was patient loyalty, especially with the insured population. All of the issues they spoke about are common in other industries. It was immediately obvious that we could help them like we had done elsewhere. The good thing was that they were hungry to implement best practice, whatever it looked like. They had a team of people working on these issues across the system, but Rhonda took the lead in the day-to-day operations and quickly became the top protégé. My right hand on the project was Joanne Earnshaw, and we made sure to give the team as much as they could handle. Rhonda was very hungry to learn—and do!

It is perhaps the biggest flattery to see that something you helped form the foundation for has grown its own wings. Five years on, it is phenomenal what Rhonda and Greg have accomplished. They have stood firmly on the foundation and applied the learnings and stayed true to the spirit and principles of Customer Experience. Now, when I speak at conferences, our original work at the system and Rhonda's subsequent work at Community General is an oft-mentioned case study. I have learned a lot from Rhonda, too. Her travails in the trenches and her evolved applications are great examples of best practice in Customer Experience, not just in healthcare. Her results speak for themselves. She has her own cadre of protégés, of which Greg is one, who continue to spread the culture and carry it further and deeper into the organization.

Greg: Why is it that we cannot get it done even though we know what to do?

We have all worked with consultants at some point in our careers, but none of us knows why we have to use them. We are the experts at our job, right? We know what is not working. The struggle comes when we start to try and fix it. Often, we fail at this. Why is it that we cannot get it done even though we know what to do? Is it because we are trying to change the outcome without really changing our habits? Of all of the times I have worked with consultants, I have never really been given anything new. It is more of a reminder than new knowledge. That is what was different about working with Rhonda. There was a whole new approach. Through her daily examples and reminders, she taught us a new way of doing things. She was so sneaky that much of what we learned from her we thought we came up with on our own. Now, I am realizing that it was not the consultants that did not give me anything new; it was my expectation of receiving a silver bullet. I had that in mind as the role of a consultant and was closed to anything else. I now understand that often we need someone else to help us along—even when we are really good at our job.

What was required for us to reach success was a new culture. What we had wanted, and probably what Rhonda was hired to do, was for someone to come in and implement initiatives. Consultants can't tell you what to do; they can only tell you what has worked at other places. They also cannot make things stick long term. I finally understand for real change and success, consultants do not give you the answers; they show you how to find the answers.

Rhonda: In the end, I had become a Patient Experience consultant.

I remember the interview I had with the CEO. Not purposefully, but maybe I was not honest with him that day. I told him a lot of ideas that I would put in place. That is probably why he hired me—because I had good ideas. I did not know during that interview about the thick steel door I was going to run smack dab into. This has been the most challenging and the most rewarding and definitely the most satisfying place I have ever worked. The most challenging because I found myself over and over not knowing what to do; the most rewarding because it pushed me to new growth. I had to let go and accept the students when they were ready. I have never been the most patient person, and this experience tested my patience daily. It was the most satisfying because the sweetest success comes from the bitterest journey. Everything happens in life for a reason and at the right time. I always want to argue when I hear people say the timing was just not right. The timing was perfect for the lesson you needed to learn. When I was introduced to the consultants, I was unaware that I needed that experience because five years in the future I was going to face the challenge of my life, and they had a lot to teach me about how to do it.

The Lesson: What You Need to Know …

Qaalfa: A good consultant builds your independence, not your dependency.
Kalina: Ask for the right kind of help.

Not every business or manager needs help from a consultant or outsider, but do consider that you may be seen as an internal consultant to managers in your own organization. This was effectively how Rhonda was seen initially when she first went to Community General.

You probably do not need a consultant if you meet these conditions:

- You have a vision and a clear way forward.
- The big boss believes in your vision.
- You have a budget to carry out your vision.

If any of these criteria is not met, you may want to look for some help.

It is obvious that if you are unsure about how to proceed, then you need help. This is often the case for novices or even experienced managers who have run out of ideas to move things forward. The situation at the hospital system when Qaalfa and Rhonda first worked together was a combination of these two. At Community General, Greg did not have a way forward in Patient Experience.

Outside help often brings fresh perspectives and tools to help you define and articulate your vision and way forward. This one is perhaps most obvious; nevertheless, when talking to potential outside help, look for the following:

- Simplicity: They should be able to explain complex concepts simply.
- Clients: They should have a client list that allows them to bring applied best practice to you.
- Adaptable approach: You may be tempted to want to hear the consultant play back the vision from the start, but the truth is your consultants should be offering you the approach to the answer, not the answer itself. At the same time, they should be willing to take some guidance from you on the shape of the vision to meet your internal reality—an effective tool is an adaptive tool. Solutions need to be realistic and applicable to your context. As much as it may be comforting to hear a consultant say he or she has all the answers, beware. The best consultants have an approach that can define those answers. Run as fast as you can if the consultant has all of the answers before you even start the project. They should be open about their blind spots.
- Emotional journey: They should make ample use of storytelling; this does not mean they just need to use examples. Rather, they need to be able to put their work in a more concrete context so that you can visualize the journey (including the emotional journey) they will lead. Like any learning situation and potential career-defining exercise, there will be moments of frustration and nervousness. The consultant should be able to describe these ahead of time. Stories are an easy vehicle for this sort of information to come out. It is hoped you see evidence of the power of storytelling in the way we wrote this book.
- Industry expertise: You may be tempted to stay within your sector. This is not wrong per se, but think if all the best practice is found within your sector.
  - If you are a novice, it will be comforting to know that the consultants specialize in your industry.
  - If you have some experience, have been to the conferences, and have the T-shirt, you will likely be in a better position to appreciate how learning from other industries will be an advantage for you.
- Technology: Technological solutions can sound like a great fix, and they are usually useful, but they are generally only enablers of cultural transformation. You can achieve cultural transformation without heavy investment in technology. Never assume that whatever is required of the people who will have to use the information technology system will do so naturally.
- Onboarding: Because people are involved, any approach needs to address how management and employees will be brought into the fold. Often, training the staff seems like the obvious solution to gaining engagement and creating

influencers; unfortunately, it is not that easy. Your consultants should offer you an approach that has built in a heavy dosage of employee buy-in to raise awareness, discussion, and collaborative solution making. This should be infused in their approach. It should not feel like an "add-on." It may be referred to as training, coaching, works hopping, and so on. It does not matter; the purpose is what matters. Even Rhonda's skills lab was just one part of an assortment of activities aimed at engaging the employee (i.e., the Engagement Bowtie).

Even if you know what you would like to do, you will have no joy if the higher-ups do not understand the significance of your approach. In this instance, one of two things can be wrong: (1) Your approach is actually not that great; or (2) the higher-ups are underdeveloped in their thinking. You need to find out which is true. This means you have to be open to the notion that the problem may be your understanding. Here, you need the following:

- Assessment: You will want them to offer a full picture of where the organization is according to a variety of enablers. If the assessment shows you that
  - Your vision is the issue, then see point 1.
  - The issue is with the higher-ups' lack of understanding, then you may need help with sending the message of your vision or with executive development. The former can probably be done in relatively short order. The latter will likely take a bit of time as it requires a mindset transformation in the boardroom.
- Show integrity: No one wants to hear that his or her baby is ugly. You need a consultant who can deliver a strong, clear message to the organization about what is going on and will affect the chances for success. The consultants need to be cool under pressure and reassuring. You need a consultant with integrity.

Finally, a common situation is that the business allocates little budget or resource to Patient Experience. In this situation, you have three choices:

- Attempt to secure more resource from the organization. This is probably what you will immediately be thinking of securing. While this is possible, it depends in large part on the mindset of the senior executives. If they feel that the Patient Experience is a top strategic imperative, then they will allocate some resources to making it happen. The consultant should be able to help you build a business case by giving you some pointers. In the end, the higher-ups may not be able to allocate all that you think is required, however. The business may not be able to afford it. In this case, see the next point.
- Become more efficient about how you are approaching the Patient Experience program. This is probably what the organization assumes needs to happen. It is one of the ways a consultant should be able to help you most. A good

consultant should be able to offer a number of options that can work within your budget. You may not obtain all that you desire given your limited resource situation, but the consultant should help you set your priorities and suggest a resource-appropriate solution.

■ Stop. Get the organization to admit that it is not serious about Patient Experience improvement, and that it cannot be done in an effective way without appropriate resources. Opt out if you think the organization is not serious about moving forward in a meaningful way. A good consultant would be able to help you get a feel for this during initial talks, but you will have to decide this one for yourself.

The main point of asking for help is to learn to fish. Likewise, the main point in achieving Customer Experience excellence through cultural transformation is teaching the organization how to fish.

Epilogue: One Year Later—Making It Stick Even When It Gets Sticky

Rhonda: It's a never-ending story.

I received an e-mail advertising the conference where Greg and I shared our story the year before. It made me reflect on the high we felt at that time. Since our return from the conference, there have been many ups and downs. We lost some very valuable leadership. Some were courted away by other hospitals, and some left for family obligations. Either way, it was difficult when the leaders left. We had the first hit to our patient safety results in two years. There were some financial and patient satisfaction setbacks as well. There were always challenges, but we knew how to roll with the punches now. We were not victims of our circumstances; we were champions of solving problems.

Walking down the hallway, you could feel the culture. I loved talking with the patients now. They made comments about how they could tell we all wanted to help them and described us as friendly. In talking with staff, everyone realized their contribution to the greater good. You never heard anyone say they were just a housekeeper anymore. Everyone knew they were valuable.

It is really simple the way you make it stick. You never set your sights on a finish line. It is not a destination that you are trying to reach. It is funny that when we started all of this, we were looking for a finish. Well, if a hospital is ever finished, then it is closed, right? More than about reaching the finish, it is about continuing the journey and evolving when needed. Now, we realize it is not about reaching the end but about creating a culture where we continue to grow to avoid the end.

Index